TITANIA'S MAGICAL COMPENDIUM

TITANIA'S MAGICAL COMPENDIUM

SPELLS AND RITUALS TO BRING A LITTLE MAGIC INTO YOUR LIFE

TITANIA HARDIE

PHOTOGRAPHS BY SARA MORRIS

THUNDER BAY
P·R·E·S·S
San Diego, California

THUNDER BAY
P · R · E · S · S

Thunder Bay Press
An imprint of the Advantage Publishers Group
5880 Oberlin Drive, San Diego, CA 92121-4794
www.thunderbaybooks.com

TEXT © Titania Hardie 2003
PHOTOGRAPHS © Sara Morris 2000/2002
LAYOUTS © Quadrille Publishing Limited 2003

All notations of errors or omissions should be addressed to Thunder Bay Press, Editorial Department, at the above address. All other correspondence (author inquiries, permissions) concerning the content of this book should be addressed to Quadrille Publishing Limited, Alhambra House, 27-31 Charing Cross Road, London WC2H 0LS, UK. E-mail: enquiries@quadrille.co.uk

Library of Congress Cataloging-in-Publication Data

Hardie, Titania.
   Titania's magical compendium : spells and rituals to bring a little magic into your life/
Titania Hardie ; photographs by Sara Morris.
      p. cm.
   Includes index.
   ISBN 1-59223-144-6
      1. Magic. 2. Witchcraft. I. Title.

BF1611.H235 2003
133.4'3--dc21

2003054043

Printed in China

1 2 3 4 5 07 06 05 04 03

INTRODUCING WHITE MAGIC. You are invited to a witches' tea party. My own favorite brew is Earl Grey, but do please join me with a cup of whatever you prefer. Tie a purple ribbon around your cup—you will understand why within a few pages!

As we make the journey through this book—and thereby through the philosophy and observance of Wicca custom—it is important to understand two basic truths. There is no room in the true witch's thoughts for arrogance toward others' religious beliefs, for all approaches to contemplating the divine, creative force are considered valid and honorable; no one should believe that their own approach is the only justified belief system. Then, too, it is vital to understand that if we as individuals have a right to happiness here on earth, now—as indeed does everyone else—we cannot contravene this spiritual truth by seeking our own pleasure and wishes at the cost of anyone else's. This demands that no individual be on the receiving end of our angry spells, or that we direct "bad feeling" to others—no matter how great we may feel the provocation to be. The only way in which the true Wicca creed allows for "revenge" over others is by our surpassing those who have done or wished us harm. In other words, think not of getting even, but rather of leaving petty-minded people far behind by attracting a much stronger and beneficial magic to ourselves. ALWAYS REMEMBER THIS CREED.

Practical magic celebrates the belief that we are all a part of the "WEB OF LIFE," and that every independent entity is connected in the minutest ways to other entities by an imperceptible web of vibrations. When we perform a small, symbolic task, it is connected to the real object of our thought by these interlaced vibrations. Quite simply, the more we are in tune with these vibratory waves, the more we can effect changes (even if very small ones) in material events. If someone wishes us negativity, persistent, positive thought returned to them will, little by little, alter their negative feelings. If someone is ill, our bold, optimistic thought can alleviate their condition to some extent. If we are out of touch with others, setting our thoughts in motion can eventually cause a chain of response. Never let negative thought, or disbelief, dissuade you!

This book is an attempt to tutor those who are willing to make these vibratory connections in their lives, and to alter their course. Hopefully, along the way some lessons will emerge about "gaining wisdom"—recognizing what we may influence, and when to leave well enough alone. It is vital to understand this: it is sometimes crucial not to intervene in personal affairs. This is a subtle point, but should have been grasped by the time we reach the final pages.

INTRODUCING THE MAGICAL CYCLE OF LIFE. Our ancestors saw the calendar of our days and hours as marking points on a great wheel of life. The perpetuation of our species was dependent upon a close relationship with the natural cycles of time: marking the seasons, understanding the pull of the moon, celebrating the power of the sun. These cycles were seen, poetically, as phases in harmony with the birth, the life, the death, and the rebirth of the goddess, primarily, and of the god, too. For a harmonious existence, it was important to shadow these moments—"AS ABOVE, SO BELOW."

Witches work closely with the "old way" of looking at things; it recognizes the natural rhythms of the earth and the natural high and low points of the seasons and the planets. Rather than seeing the earth simply as gas, rock and water, it is an invitation to see it still as a mother-nurturer—our home. To keep the world turning happily, and to encourage the return of the waning sun and the correct behavior at the dying year, the force of "earth magic" was employed. This was to caress the little midpoints—like spokes in the wheel of the year—into their next forward movement.

Those midpoints are the solar and the lunar festivals— or sabbats. The Winter Solstice is the shortest day of the year, measuring the happy moment from which the sun will grow stronger again. This is December 21st in the northern hemisphere (Yule) and June 21st in the southern. At the Spring Equinox, day and night are of equal length—just as they are at the Autumn Equinox. In the north, the Spring Equinox is March 21st and the Autumn Equinox is September 21st, whereas in the southern hemisphere, again, those dates are reversed. The Summer Solstice, of course, is the longest day—June 21st for dwellers in the north, and December 21st for Antipodeans.

The lunar festivals retain their Celtic names, and these mark the moon's most important cycles. Samhain, also called Hallowe'en, is the start of winter, the Celtic New Year, and it equates to the so-called "dark moon." This is October 31st. Beltane, also called "May Day," is its opposite, and celebrates the arrival of summer—the full moon. This is May 1st. Imbolc is the first day of spring—very early spring—and equates to the waxing (or growing) moon. This is February 1st. Its coordinate point is August 1st, the festival of Lughnasadh (pronounced *loonassa*), which initiates the start of the autumnal moon, or the waning moon. The Christian names of Lammas (for Lughnasadh) and Candlemas (for Imbolc) may be more familiar.

Together we can quietly inject magic into all the days of our lives, surviving low tides and riding triumphant on high ones. We will carry our own inner sunshine through wintry chill, and keep cool and relaxed with magical awareness through the sun's zenith at high summer. We will live close to the earth's pulse. We will learn how to live in greater harmony withth the earth and our neighbours, and understand how to admire her amazing treasures, and use them more wisely. BLESSED BE.

MASTER SPELL: **A MAGIC CIRCLE.** This is the most important precursor of powerful magic. The idea of the circle is to create a powerful zone into which nothing harmful can reach. From inside the 360 degrees, the powerful witch has control over any forces coming from any direction: her sphere of power reaches everywhere. Most importantly, the circle also prevents any curious lower spirits from entering into the magic making and corrupting the results.

There are many variations on the construction of the magic circle. However, some of the descriptions derive from the Druidic tradition, which, it is widely believed, sometimes used a circle in connection with divine sacrifice. From the Wiccan creed of harming no one, and my grandmother's beautiful circle—which was literally a pool of light and accompanied all her incantations for healing heart, mind, and body—I draw my own preferred model for a magic circle from which to pour forth beautiful, powerful, enlightened thoughts. To do it justice, you may wish to use as many as forty or fifty candles for a circle about two yards in diameter! If this seems too extravagant, settle for thirteen, and place them equidistantly around your drawn circle.

YOU WILL NEED
At least 13 small candles in glass holders, either flame-red or white (or both); rose petals, or rose potpourri, to strew in the center, with a little rose oil added to intensify the fragrance; a handful of earth; a small dish of water; a small mirror; a birch leaf, or twig if it is winter; a twig or leaf from the appropriate tree for the moon/month in which you are performing this spell; 2 yards of flame-red ribbon.

MOON PHASE: *Full (birch moon, for the purist).*

Choose carefully the area in which you are to create your circle. It is best to use the floor area in a room where you will habitually perform your magic, or even your garden on a still night.

Standing in the center of the circle you will create, place the candles around it in a clockwise direction—no more than 18 inches apart, and much closer if you are prepared to buy more candles and create a really intense ring of fire. Still standing in the center, strew some rose petals or potpourri around your feet, and sprinkle with a little rose oil to make the scent very powerful. Step once outside the circle, and place in the north of it the earth, in the south of it the dish of water, and west of center the mirror, which you should first hold up to the moon for just a few seconds. Finally, place the leaf (twig), or leaves (twigs), within the circle.

As soon as you are ready to begin the magic ritual of cleansing and bringing in power to your art, girdle yourself with the flame-red ribbon and tie it at your waist with a large bow. Now raise your arms to the moon, entreating also the element of air to carry your thought waves and draw down the strength and luminosity of the beautiful full moon into your circle. Allow the light to fill your own being, and feel your emotional tides rising with the moon's energy. Now bow once to the divine entity, and promise to make only magic that is good.

MOON CYCLES

WORKING MAGIC BY THE MOON

WE

SHOULD BEGIN OUR JOURNEY BY

UNDERSTANDING THE IMPORTANCE OF THE MOON

AND HOW TO WORK OUR MAGIC IN TUNE WITH HER CYCLES.

IN ITALIAN WITCHCRAFT, ARADIA IS QUEEN OF THE WITCHES, BESTOWER

OF WISDOM AND SECRETS. DAUGHTER OF THE MOON AND THE SUN, SHE IMPARTS

CELESTIAL KNOWLEDGE TO THOSE WITH A WISE MIND AND A COURAGEOUS HEART.

THE OWL AND THE HARE ARE HER NIGHT MESSENGERS. WITCHES RECOGNIZE THE

IMPORTANCE OF FLOWING WITH NATURE'S RHYTHMS, SEEING IN OUR OWN NATURE THE

REFLECTION OF THE MOON'S ORBIT AROUND THE SUN (ROUGHLY 28 DAYS, WITH A STRONG

CONNOTATION FOR WOMEN) AND THE EARTH'S ROTATION ACROSS ONE YEAR. KNOWING

THAT THE MOON RULES THE TIDES AND BEING OURSELVES MADE UP OF A HIGH

CONTENT OF WATER, WE CAN MAXIMIZE THE ENERGY OF OUR LIVES BY

UNDERSTANDING THIS LUNAR INFLUENCE. AS THE MOON WAXES FROM

DARKNESS TO BRIGHTNESS, THEN WANES TO DARKNESS AGAIN, THE

CYCLE OF HUMAN LIFE——BIRTH, ADOLESCENCE, ADULTHOOD,

DEATH, THEN REBIRTH——ARE REFLECTED AND

UNDERSTOOD.

NEW MOON

The waxing, growing moon brings moisture, the rising tide, and the flow of all life. This is especially so with plant life; the first 14 days of the moon's cycle are the best time for sowing seeds, giving tiny plants the opportunity to swell and ripen with the waxing moon. We, too, feel a quickening with the growing moon. The brand-new moon, lasting only a day, is sometimes obscured by the light of the sun, making a vague outline. Women often feel vulnerable and emotional at this time.

Under the dreamy spell of the "maiden moon," Diana in her first blush of maidenhood is the clearest example of growing potential. This is the moment for a spell dedicated to a new beginning in love, work, or home. This most open moment of consciousness is also a good time to meditate, as you will be at your most receptive. Be ready for inspirational thought.

For a "new moon" spell you need gossamer-thin threads, the silver hoarfrost or silky snail trails of nature. Stand before a silvery web to speak your intent toward a new project or person in your life. Dress in white like invisible silvery light. Talk to the east, where sun and moon both rise. If a snail has left its trail, or the frost has kissed the grass around you with silvery breath, address Diana and her daughter, Aradia. Ask for feminine inspiration, crystal-clear vision and understanding, the blossoming of new thoughts. Ask for help in launching one new project, and the goddess will hear you.

CRESCENT MOON

This is the first obvious appearance of the waxing moon, as it begins to swell in its outline beyond the new moon toward the first quarter. Look for this pretty moon in the afternoon sky toward the setting sun, lasting for several days.

This is the moon of continuing dedication, treated magically like the new moon. The waxing energy is conducive to growing thought and inspiration; personal energy is also waxing. For the first 14 days we are at peak energy to begin new projects and carry them through.

Continue ritual for a new opening—perhaps working a spell that unfolds over seven days—and incorporate young plant seedlings. Place a sprig of foliage in a silver ring by a white candle, with an invocation stating your desire for new things. Tend it for seven days, as near as possible to the appearance of the crescent, late in the afternoon. Anything you ask for in an unselfish way will be granted as the moon continues to wax.

WAXING HALF MOON

The first quarter, or half moon, occurs about one week after the new moon. Now you can see the moon from noon to about midnight, connecting it with the field of dreams. You should conceptualize the growing tangibility of your magic making and wishes—try to surround things important to you with beautiful, bright silver light in your mind's eye, so you may learn something intuitive to help you in that area. Actual messages that point you in a very important direction may suddenly materialize.

Progress from verbal magic, where you speak your wishes (called invocation) to thought—practice holding one idea in your mind for several minutes without chatter. While looking at the moon for a few minutes, visualize the appearance of amazing things in your life: achievements, social harmony, success in work, growing love relationships, possibly fertility, or finding a happy home. See your plans forming into actualities against the half circle now brightly visible in the sky. Whisper words, and be gentle and soft-spoken with your friends.

GIBBOUS MOON

The last slip-thread before the moon is truly full, this beautiful
moon rises near sunset and is full of promise. This is the last
moment before peak fertility at full moon. Close your eyes and
let your mind drift back to a moment that made you truly happy.
If this makes you smile, wish upon the moon and your full,
fecund power of imagination to open up many new moments of
future true happiness.

Your emotions are at full tilt now, so this is a perfect
time for casting deep love spells, or magic connected with
relationships or fertility. Open your eyes to the light of the
moon, and say: *"Diana (or Tana, or indeed another variant is
Titania, or Selene), spirit of the moon, With your deep
understanding of the souls of men and women, Beautiful Diana,
by the reverence I give thee, And the joy of love which you have ever
seen and known, Guardian of our secret thought and nighttime
hopes: Grant me aid in my love, and my heart's fond desire, which I
do swear will cause harm unto none. So mote it be."* (It is perfectly
acceptable to read this out from the book, under the light of the
moon with a candle, rather than trying to memorize it.) Now
place a silver talisman of a dog, an owl, or a hare—the
messengers of the moon—up to the moon's glow. See the moon's
face transform into the face of your loved one, and express your
true emotion to them in your mind's eye, but only in a whisper.
Place the talisman near a candle and a mirror which can reflect
just a tiny ray of the moon's light. As the full moon arrives, your
powers in love should prosper.

FULL MOON

This is the full face of the gracious lady moon, also called the
astral moon, which rises as the sun sets and sets as he rises. The
long, brightly moonlit night casts "moonshadow" and is ideal for
promoting astral travel and psychic dreams. This time embodies
the psyche of opposites, turning things around and invoking
the greatest power of the mother moon, now in her zenith as
maternal figure. The emotional highs associated with this moon
have long been connected with mental imbalance (hence the
terms "moonstruck" and "lunatic"). However, if you can balance
your deeply enriched feeling power with your acute psychic
awareness and inner consciousness, this is the moon to work the
most powerful magic, to send messages far away and be
telepathically at your peak.

Make magic for powerful love and passion, or to
communicate with someone who is away from you or not
speaking to you as you would wish. Reflect this "below" (on
earth) by putting scent on your pulse, lighting many candles, and
putting a photo of someone dear in the center of them. Place an
emblem of communication alongside—anything from a pen to a
cell phone!

MOON DREAMS

If the moon speaks to you in symbols, she often shows you
flowers. If you experience heavily scented flowers, you must grasp
an opportunity that is offered you. If you see yourself gathering
flowers, you will have a nice surprise or be successful. If you see
flowers gathered into a basket or vase, a new love is growing and
you may hear of a wedding. If you see yourself floating over
moonlit gardens, this is a general blessing and sign of luck.

DISSEMINATING MOON

The moon is now on the wane. Unlike the moisture-bringing waxing moon, this moon is drying, governing the ebb of the tides and of plant saps, so this is the time for harvesting crops and cutting flowers. The disseminating moon also takes away the extreme feelings of yesterday's full moon, the emotional tide gently ebbing away from the high pulse point.

The moon is now visible from about an hour after sunset well into midmorning, which makes her a good confidante for an honest self-view. Think of yourself, your direction, your present position, and discuss this with the midmorning moon over a cup of coffee.

Now is the time for working spells of reflection and deep thoughts. On a physical level it is the perfect time to go on a cleansing diet or detox program, as your body will not retain fluids as much as it does with the growing moon. If you have a one- to two-week healthy-eating regime planned, start on the disseminating moon and you'll be twice as likely to stick with it.

WANING HALF MOON

Now half light and half dark in the circle, the moon in its last quarter will appear around midnight and be visible well into the daytime, until roughly noon. This is still the moon of reflection and meditative thought, but it is used to work magic to rid ourselves of unwanted elements, which we demand to float away on the ebbing tide. Make circles in the early morning under the still-visible moon in a "widdershins" direction (counterclockwise). Turn your body thrice, pausing at each revolution. Carry a magnet and hold it away from your body. Invoke the negative element/virus/person to depart from you in peace. Present the magnet to the moon, then place it outside your house or near the front door of your apartment, but hang it points down (not points up like a horseshoe whose luck you wish to preserve). Under the moon's darkness, in seven days, you will bury the magnet (see page 19).

WANING CRESCENT MOON

This is the daytime moon, the last slip of moon seen early in the
morning, rising just before the sunrise and not setting until later
in the afternoon. This moon, also known as the "balsamic" or
"crone" moon, is almost dark and is dedicated to the crone or
wise woman, who knows all from the darker worlds. She is the
most mature and wise of the three-personed goddess: the maiden
who was new, the mother who was full, and now the crone—the
sibyl who sees both the future and deep into the hearts of men,
knowing all, understanding what to change and what to leave be.
This, then, is the moon of mystery, and she watches over our
rituals of divination and inner knowledge. She will help you to
let go of things that no longer serve a useful purpose in your
life—whether you want to give up smoking, quit a job, or
leave a lover. Look to the wise goddess face of the crone moon
to understand unfathomed elements—to inquire of oracles or
to direct your dreams to give the most complex and personal
of answers.

DARK MOON

Just before the new moon appears there are a couple of days
when the moon is virtually invisible. This is the dark moon,
when it has waned almost away. Now is the time to turn
completely inward and heal aspects of the self that require greater
understanding. When we are in error, we need to think deeply
and draw on unsilenced voices for an awareness of our
obligations. This moment is apt to think on those dearest to us
who have left us, to speak out to the ghosts of our past and wish
them well, to place flowers on graves. Also, since this is the moon
of the dark, we need self-honoring rituals to give us strength and
confidence, for this is often the darkest personal moment of the
month, "the dark night of the soul, just before the dawn."

Make your own moon magic now: sleep under a crystal,
or find a round light with a moonlike shape which can lend us
illumination. This is also the time to bury a magnet that has
demagnetized negativity: this is the ritual you might already
have begun (see page 16). Rid yourself of the bad feeling of a
problem—such as illness or ill feeling from another person—by
burying the magnet you have worked on for several days under
a powerful tree such as an oak or an ash. Wish anyone involved
in the bad feeling well, in another direction, as you go. Spend the
last day of the dark moon in a personal reverie, quietly thinking,
rather than being noisy and high-spirited—which behavior
belongs instead to (and should be elicited by) the full moon.

IN THE BEGINNING

BIRCH MOON

The witches' calendar year is based on the moon cycles, so divides into thirteen "months," each of which is ruled by a tree. The first moon, the moon of beginning, is ruled by the birch, and in this chapter we introduce the components that are required to start practicing white magic. The elements of earth, air, fire, and water are explained. We learn to work magic by the moon's clock and discover how to weave magical ritual and thought into everyday life without drawing attention to it. The significance of colors, scents, and oils is touched upon, although it will be further developed in subsequent chapters, and we learn about some of the tools of magic making. We look at the calendar significance of this first moon, covering the period late December to mid-January, and of Yule, the festival that falls in this period. Honoring this ancient festival can increase all our luck and happiness in small things. The master spell draws blessings from the birch moon and tree and, if done once or twice a year, will bring joy and luck into your life.

BIRCH MOON—MOON OF BEGINNING. Color: FLAME-RED. Scent: ROSE. Number: 1. We must begin at the beginning and draw our first lesson in magic making in partnership with the first Druidic moon and all her domain, for it is the moon that introduces us to the infancy of magic.

"I saw the new moon late yestreen
   Wi' the auld moon in her arm;
   And if we gang to sea, master,
   I fear we'll come to harm."
"SIR PATRICK SPENS"—ANONYMOUS

The birch tree, which Samuel Coleridge dubbed the *"lady of the wood,"* is associated with purification and the protection of children and dependants. The beautiful silvery appearance of the trunk has an affinity with the silvery moon and reflects the moonlight at night, giving the tree an ethereal, very magical dimension. Perhaps it is for this reason that the witch's broom—symbol of her power and magical energy—was made from birch twigs, and sweeping the area in which you will perform magical rites with the birch broom, or "besom," is a powerful way to influence the outcome of your spell making.

HONORING THE BIRCH

We must now consider briefly the significance of the birch in the calendar, and ways to honor and celebrate both season and tree-spirit. The moon itself falls just after Yule (December 21), and runs from approximately December 25 to January 17. This means that New Year's is the festival associated with the birch moon, the first moon of the year, while the elder governs Yule itself.

You can reasonably weave some old pagan Yule rituals into any other religious feasts that likewise straddle midwinter (midsummer in the southern hemisphere) and the turn of a new year—remember how the Yule log, wreath, and charms placed in the Christmas pudding, in England, to ensure a bountiful year ahead have been incorporated into the Christian observance of Christmas. Indeed, the correspondence between the Christian festival and Yule/New Year's could not be more apparent, as the old festival was an honoring of the "new life" of the sun, which is born immediately after the Winter Solstice, December 21, which is why Christmas Day was set at this same moment in the calendar.

Two adversaries battle for leadership at Yuletide: namely, the Oak King, who is the manifestation of the summery, waxing year, and the Holly King, who is the spirit of the waning, wintry year. Connections between the appearance and accoutrements of the Holly King—who drove a team of deer, the animal sacred to the Celtic gods and the Druids, and wore holly in his hat—and Father Christmas, or Santa Claus, are easy to make. Even the red candles we use at Christmas have a connection with the color of the first flame of the sun and the color associated with the first, birch moon. Candles of this color—along with white, which symbolizes all unity and thus the full return and restart of the wheel of the year—often adorned the altars and feast tables in the Yuletide house, much as they do now. The birch, however, is the symbolic tree of renewal and purification, and you might include birch twigs in your Yule fires to deepen the tie between the dying year (elder) and the reborn year (birch). The beautiful birch is a goddess tree, slender and silvery, and a symbol of hope of the summer returning. When the tree bursts into foliage later in the year, keep a sprig as a talisman for luck, love, and protection, and wear it pinned to your coat on May Day, at midsummer, at Lammas (August 1) and again at Yule. As the birch tree is loved by the fairies, cherishing a birch twig or sprig may give the wearer help in seeing these folk.

WORKING MAGIC BY THE MOON'S CLOCK

The birch moon is also known as the moon of inception and falls immediately after Yule. The moon is measured from full, which is the zenith of its power. This means, too, that magic is worked from the full moon through a waning moon (a moon on its way from full to last quarter, or last quarter to the day before "new"), which is used to rid a situation of bad spirit or feeling; and then through the growing (waxing) moon, which is used to attract new, better, growing opportunities. Choose the timing of your magic-making very carefully. . . .

THE MOON PHASE

If this is to be your first foray into spell making, you should begin with a splash! Build up to your first magic: you need not wait for the birch moon in late December/early January, but it would be wonderful to start on a full moon, when the celestial body exerts its most powerful pull on the earth, its oceans, and all of us, whose being is so largely made up of water. Most calendars have moon information printed on the appropriate days. Check which moon will begin with the next full moon, and honor it in your magic making with a twig from the appropriate tree, as well as a birch twig to signify your own beginning as a magic-worker.

If you are absolutely longing to start but have just missed a full moon, all is not lost. So long as you work with a waning moon for purification spells, you are still using the potent power of moon magic to rid yourself of anything negative. Always use a waning moon in any spell that banishes something—be it a wart or a smoking habit, weight loss, or a sweet ex-lover who cannot accept your new relationship (this last should be a very tender spell!). You should use the waxing moon only when you want to draw something into your life.

WEATHER

At times when you cannot use a full moon—wait for a storm! There is no more electric moment at which to launch your magic thought into the world than with the birth of a storm of rain and wind, and a ragged moon. You can bring these elements together in one extraordinary way, if you are lucky enough to see "the new moon with the old moon in her arms." This happens when the part of the moon covered by the shadow of the earth is seen through it—rimmed with a silver thread, in effect. In Scotland, for instance, this is regarded as an infallible portent of bad weather, and occurs just before the storm is about to break.

Keep beautiful, sunlit days for spells of healing and love: the gentle solar rays will soften your energy and transmit warmth automatically with your own message.

THE ELEMENTS. Our strong personal connection to all other matter can be achieved through our understanding that we are all made up of the four elements —EARTH, AIR, FIRE, and WATER—one or other in greater proportion than others. Fire is the principal element in magic for its connection with creativity and purification; Water is the other principal element, for as human beings we are made up more of water than of any other element; and then, too, it is the element of emotion! Earth is vital to magic, for it is our planetary home; and everything we wish to "reach" must reverberate through the air. Weave them all in.

FIRE

Fire is one of the crucial four elements, connected indissolubly with the "divine spark." Representative of the sun's life-giving energy, it has transfiguring powers. Light is connected with knowledge and a move away from fear; heat has the power to drive off illness and create mood and closeness with another being; and flame purifies, regenerates, and creates chemical changes. Fire changes raw food to cooked, removing much of its impurity, and fire applied to cold water gives us warm water in which to bathe. Quite simply, fire refines us.

By thinking in a concentrated manner over a candle, and then lighting it, we symbolically move our thought out beyond us, into the ether. The power of thought is the linchpin of magic, for it is through thought that we gain mastery over the situations and other life forms around us.

Part of the way in which magic works is by enacting an affinity between people and things. Lighting a sacred flame calls down a piece of the powerful sun to shine on a benevolent situation, or "burn up" destructive forces which are hindering individual progress. This lies at the heart of the magic flame circle of purification.

COLORS AND CANDLES

As the bringers of light and color and, sometimes, scent, candles are an essential part of magic making. We are all familiar with the use of wax in images and figurines as part of the myth of witches' work, but the pure and untainted candle to which a thought and wish is attached is a powerful carrier of messages. It is important to have a wide range of candles available, for the many different purposes they fulfill in magic ritual. Keep a rainbow of colors, and always choose the color appropriate to the subject (you can check individual chapters for these). Always place a candle on your altar to correspond to the moon and month you are in, and work one or more colors in tandem as necessary.

For initiating magic, the color you need is flame-red. If you were trying, for instance, to precipitate some love interest for the first time with someone you like, you would use the red to initiate communication, and marry it to purple (for passion) or pink (for love), in addition to the appropriate color for the month.

For working steady magic, use votive candles in glass holders; these will burn for up to about eleven hours. If you buy "tea-lights" (very small candles that burn for just a few hours), you will have only a short time for your magic to work.

This is fine if you have a short spell to perform, or once you have become adept at sending your thoughts and getting quick results—in other words, after much practice. Until that time, use the longer-burning candles, to which you can return many times over several hours and re-send the thoughts of your spell. The use of "column candles" (the really big, church-style candles which can burn for days) and tapers should be matched to particular spells. When you are burning a candle and working a spell over several days, and notching the candle in several places to mark each day's burning, a taper in the appropriate color is the right choice.

If you are selecting a candle for an altar—one that will last for several weeks or even remain indefinitely—use a pillar candle in white or beeswax, and add one smaller candle in the color appropriate to the moon and month.

SCENT

Many candles can now be bought with essential oils already incorporated into them, and this makes lighter work for a witch. Scent is vital in spell making for several reasons: it alters the psychological state of the worker, bestowing confidence, for instance, or aiding concentration; it affects the mood of the recipient of magic in love or healing spells, relaxing them or reviving their spirits; and it reminds us of times and places that may be helpful to our focus, as well as working again on the affinities between people and things.

There is an equivalent olfactory "rainbow" which can and should be woven into magic, and each chapter in the book specifies the scent that corresponds to that moon and month. If you cannot find candles that are ready-scented with appropriate fragrances (not "ice-cream sundae" or "chocolate fudge"), you can instead anoint the candle yourself with oils (perfume or essential) from your storage cupboard. The easiest way to do this is to light the candle first and wait until the wax has become a little molten at the top. Extinguish the flame, add a few drops of oil to the wax and allow it to harden again, then re-light the wick. The same result can be achieved by softening the edges of the candle with a flame, rolling it in some oil, waiting for the wax to harden, and then lighting the candle.

For any magic purification ritual, rose is the absolutely essential oil. It should be burned with the candle—for extra effect, this can be in a burner alongside the candle on your altar. If you feel like creating a proper piece of theater, burn some rose potpourri on a charcoal burner or in a fireplace to cleanse and purify completely both the environment and any situation.

THE OTHER ELEMENTS

These will come under closer inspection in later chapters, but deserve a mention here.

WATER, the element of feeling, is used in the spell of purification and can be represented by placing clean river or rainwater in a silver or wooden dish beside your magic-working area, or on the altar. Some spells require that you go to water to perform them.

EARTH, the element of humankind (from which we are made, although we are made also from water) is crucial to the "grounding" of a spell—that is, making it real and not just wishful thinking. Some spells require symbolic burial to make use of earth; otherwise, a handful of earth, or plants grown in earth, will find their way into magic ritual.

AIR is all around us, and drawing our arms up or breathing steadily during magic making will involve the air—the element of our thought. Some spells are best performed from a height to make full use of the air.

MAGIC IN EVERYDAY LIFE. As you begin to walk the path of Wicca philosophy, you will want to incorporate magic and spell making into your daily life, but perhaps without drawing attention to it. Because spell making is as fundamental to Wicca as the air that we breathe, finding an outward expression of magic will draw more power, merriment, and joy into your life. The aim is to bring a rainbow of colors into your life—perhaps without anyone else realizing—and subsequently find a *"pot of gold"* within your everyday existence.

OUTSIDE

OPEN YOUR HEART TO NATURE. Vow to think more about the natural world, and make your home (whatever its type) a haven for living things. If you live in an apartment, this will be somewhat restricted, but you can nevertheless make sure of keeping as many thriving potted plants, herbs, and flowers—of varied colors—close to as many sunlit windows as possible. Whenever you water them, simply say *"Blessed Be,"* and think warmly of all animated nature.

GO FURTHER: cast crumbs to birds from your rooftop, leave out old bread, even provide proper seed in suitable containers through the winter. If you have a garden, or a balcony, make a birdhouse or nesting box to encourage wildlife around your living quarters. A bird bath, or a water feature that will attract dragonflies and other watery life, brings the element of water to add to the element of air that your birdlife symbolizes. Thank the deity every day for these simple pleasures of sharing moments with other creatures and plants. Think of it as an offering to Mother Nature to place these items, which will attract her progeny, around your environment. Tie white and purple ribbons around your front-door knob, gatepost, or mailbox, or even your car steering wheel, to protect you and your loved ones and draw beneficence to your dwelling. Always feel a rush of color entering your life as you do this.

INSIDE

Make sure you have all the colors of the rainbow somewhere in your home. Venerate the element of fire with a constant candle flame or altar. Spread a cloth over a beautiful table or even an old box (either is fine) in any color that relates to the season, or tree/moon, or just your own mood. Place a cut flower in a glass vase (symbolizing light), or a growing plant in a small terracotta pot (symbolizing earth), on this altar, and light a candle for even just a few moments whenever you are at home. Always thank the spirit for small blessings, and look for some good in everything. This simple re-attuning of your thinking to a positive outlook should gradually draw powerful good fortune to you and those dearest to you. Think this through whenever you light your flame, or pot up herbs and flower seeds, or feed the birds, or water your greenery.

RIBBONS

You will be invited to incorporate ribbon—one of magic's most significant ingredients—not only into your everyday life in the most romantic of ways, but also into many of the spells described in this book. Ribbons symbolize the beauty of a cord with other people, and I like to tie ribbons around the letters and cards I send to symbolize an offered bond of welcome, or perhaps healing, or the need for swift response, in colors that reflect the particular situation. If you also place a few drops of an appropriate essential oil on the ribbon ends, so much the better. You will find more detail about ribbons in each succeeding chapter, matching the concerns of the color and the subject.

Ribbons, then, can be tied around any object to draw magic into the situation. You will tantalize friends with questions about your decorative style if you tie a large golden yellow ribbon—which symbolizes both gatherings and celebration— around your dinner table. This is likely to lend a magic hand to the evening's proceedings, and your guest(s) will be "ENCHANTED." In addition to this, I usually buy fresh, growing herbs from the supermarket weekly and tie red ribbons around the pots or foliage. This initiates the magic vibration of the plants into the air and around my visitors. Sometimes I send every dinner guest away with an herb tied in this way, so that they take a little magic and love home with them.

AROUND YOUR HOUSE OR OFFICE, OR EVEN IN YOUR CAR, TIE RIBBONS OF DIFFERENT COLORS.

- A silvery-colored ribbon or cord, tied around the telephone, will draw happy and positive communications from friends and associates.

- Tie a green ribbon around the faucets of your bathtub, so that as you soak you draw health, mental alertness, perfection, wisdom, love, and the ability to complete simple tasks calmly into your mind, body, and spirit. Guests will also feel recharged when they go into your bathroom.

- Luck will attend you if you place sunshine-yellow candles or ribbons anywhere that money is kept: *tie a yellow ribbon around your checkbook, for example!*

- Send out cards and letters tied with a ribbon of any color to suit the situation: *green if your recipient is sick or tired, purple if you want to attract attention, pink if it's love, olive green for forgiveness, black or white for matters of destiny.*

- Tie a red ribbon around the herbs you grow on your windowsill, to spread love and happiness in your home and to increase the joy you experience from eating the herbs in salads and cooked dishes.

MASTER SPELL: TO DRAW BLESSINGS FROM THE BIRCH MOON AND TREE.

This is a simple spell to entreat joy and happiness to attend your life. It asks for nothing specific, although the concepts of renewal, hope, and infinite possibility are inextricably linked with the wishes herein. You may find that performing this spell only, once or twice a year, will circumvent the need for any spells that ask for something specific, for luck is drawn powerfully with this ritual.

This is a beautiful spell to do at any time when the birch holds sway. You should notice soon afterward that even the smallest tasks can be executed more expediently and that many things that are important to you seem to fall—magically—into place.

YOU WILL NEED

1 yard of red ribbon; a flame-red candle (choose a column or pillar candle this time, so that you may relight it for a few hours each day for 14 days—or, more correctly, nights); a long-stemmed red flower, or bouquet of flowers, placed in water; a wand cut from a birch tree (ask first!), no more than 12 inches long; a few drops of benzoin, frankincense, or rose oil, or all three (all purifying oils which also bring blessings).

MOON PHASE: *Full…or nearly so.*

At a quiet time, bow to the moon and ask attendance from the divine spirit. Tie the red ribbon into a bow around the base of the candle, and place it next to the flower or flowers on a small table. Take the wand in your dominant hand and raise your arms to the moon. Make a pledge to notice, and be concerned for, nature in any small way. Widen this thought, by all means, to the most important element of it: the pledge ultimately to do more for those around you who need your help in any form, and in any way that you can give it, according to your means. In other words, promise to venerate the one life we share with everything, which is part of the divine spark.

Anoint the candle with oil and then light it; as you do so, close your eyes and think of all the life forms breathing quietly and imperceptibly around you. Ask for help in all things, and offer thanks for all the thoughts that bring a smile to your face. Ask especially for luck and love for the children around you, and promise to try to make them smile whenever you can. Every time you raise a smile on another's face, you please the divine spirit immeasurably.

Pass the wand through the flame and in an arc around the candle; then describe a circle around your working area with the wand, moving your whole body clockwise as you do so. Say simply, *"Blessed be all things; may I add to the harmony of the life force; hold me gently in the web of all creation. So mote it be!"* Lay the wand near the candle, sing, laugh, sit, relax, and think warm and even funny thoughts about yourself and those around you. After about an hour, blow out the candle and untie the ribbon, saying *"Blessed Be"* as you do so.

You are now ready to move on to the next phase of magic making and tackle divination.

VISION

ROWAN MOON

THIS

CHAPTER EXPLORES VISUAL SYMBOLOGY

IN MAGIC. THE SIGNIFICANCE OF INDIVIDUAL SYMBOLS IS

EXPLAINED, SO THAT YOU WILL BE ABLE TO SELECT PICTORIAL

DEVICES RELEVANT TO ANY SITUATION. THUS, THIS CHAPTER REVEALS THE

IMPORTANCE OF PUTTING YOUR OWN SIGNATURE ON YOUR MAGIC MAKING AND

SHOWS YOU HOW TO BEGIN TO DO SO. THE MASTER SPELL CONCERNS ASTRAL TRAVEL

AND CLAIRVOYANCE, SO THAT WE CAN START THE PROCESS OF EMPTYING THE MIND OF

BRIC-A-BRAC AND OPENING IT TO INSPIRATIONAL POWER; THOSE WHO ARE QUICK

LEARNERS WILL ALREADY BE BEGINNING TO RECEIVE CLAIRVOYANT FLASHES ABOUT THEIR

LIFE AND FUTURE. THE "VARIATION" SPELLS INCLUDE ONE THAT EMBRACES ORDINARY

TRAVEL AND IS THE WITCH'S EQUIVALENT OF WEARING A ST. CHRISTOPHER MEDAL. WE

LOOK AT THE CALENDAR SIGNIFICANCE OF THE ROWAN MOON, WHICH INCLUDES THE

FEAST DAY OF IMBOLC, ABSORBED INTO THE CHRISTIAN CALENDAR AS

CANDLEMAS. THIS IS NOT A POWERFUL MOMENT OF EARTH ENERGY, BUT

THE FIRST SIGNS OF LIFE ARE BEGINNING TO APPEAR IN THE FORM

OF CROCUSES, DAFFODILS, AND SNOWDROPS. THE

EARTH IS STARTING TO STIR...

IMBOLC: THE EARTH STIRS. This is the festival of early spring, celebrated on February 1st/2nd, the moment when the earth reawakens. The festival of Imbolc marks the transformation of winter into earliest spring: the movement away from the sway of the crone toward the virgin goddess.

The Christianization of this festival coincides with Mary taking the infant Christ child to the temple for purification, where she was told that he would be a "light unto the world." For this reason, the Christian festival of Candlemas (symbolizing the light) was absorbed into the pagan feast day, which actually occurs on February 2. The Celtic world recalls the honor of Brigid, or Briide, the Pagan earth goddess, and this time magically belongs to the reappearing maiden goddess, who is full of sacred understanding from her time within the sleeping earth of winter. Nature heralds her return: the signs of life returning are not obvious, but they are apparent to those with careful sight who will take the trouble to notice. The springs and swelling streams are her attributes—the life-giving waters of soul and survival. There are several significant rituals to perform.

Catkins are now appearing on the trees, especially willows—this is the time to make the most important wishes of the year. On February 1st or 2nd, find a willow tree (near a river or by water in a park). Tie a love-knot into a willow frond. Celebrate a rainbow of good feeling for others by attaching seven colored ribbons of the spectrum in the pale green branches of the tree. They will flutter on the wind, bringing prayers for goodness to all you think about. Only three wishes are permitted during the year, so choose yours carefully.

As this is the festival of lights, a circle should be made of candles or tea-lights, and communion for higher inspiration should be sought from the goddess. As it is also a lunar sabbat, there is a strong association with the mysteries of the unknown. Meditation at this time will bring enlightenment and clairvoyant answers, so it is appropriate to sit in a circle of lights, meditate, sing, or chant, then ask questions of your soul that are troubling you. Answers come after a night's sleep, during which no word must be uttered.

At this time love rituals will be best applied to a very new love, or the wish to meet someone. The Imbolc maiden is innocent, but her senses are stirred and she is nubile. A shrine to love, harnessing Imbolc energy, will include attributes of femininity of the maiden: hair, ribbons, and ornaments, as well as a simple vase containing a crocus or snowdrop. Honor to the maiden goddess at this time, incorporating the symbols of the flower and a lock of female hair, will bring blessings to all under the roof. Plant one white flower (such as a rose) at this time for peace and prosperity from the maiden.

Corn dollies were the trappings of the goddesses of early spring. If you wish to bless your home, office, or bedchamber in the old way, make a corn dolly, burn candles to honor the spring spirit, and plant your spring seedlings with a short invocation to the goddess for the fruitful realization of your wishes. Also, give thanks for all blessings bestowed thus far in the year.

ROWAN MOON—MOON OF VISION AND ASTRAL TRAVEL. Color: RUBY or PINK-GOLD (colors of the winter sunset). Scent: GERANIUM. Number: 2. Visualization is a serious notion in the performance of magic and spells. Based on the contention (long held in Hindu tradition) that thoughts are the beginning of all actualization, visualizing any desired end very crisply will—ultimately—produce the materialization of that vision. Thus, the more precisely a vision can be formulated, and then held, the more perfectly will that vision become reality.

"And Winter, slumbering in the open air
 Wears on his smiling face a dream of Spring!"
"WORK WITHOUT HOPE"
SAMUEL TAYLOR COLERIDGE

If you would become an adept witch, learn the art of visualization well. The effort you make will be rewarded with an evocation to match your dream; but, of course, as always, dream (or wish) wisely!

Central to art of visualization are the rowan tree and moon. Part of the connection may be to do with the weather that occurs around this time in early February—frosts and silent nights, clear, icy skies, and frozen ground. There is a timelessness and a stillness which lend themselves naturally to the gentle internal rhythms of the psychic brain. The earth stirs into a vision of reawakening, and the first early bulbs appear above the ground. This is a metaphor of sorts for the seeds of knowledge and actual being of our future, which lie quiet and undisturbed within our subconscious until they blossom forth into colorful symbols of what will come.

Hence, the festival of Imbolc—taken from the Celtic word "imelc," meaning ewe's milk, and thus symbolic of the first few lambs of the season fed by the ewes—is a celebration of "first stirrings" and a good time to look ahead to the unfolding year. To the careless eye, there is nothing to see; to the trained eye, there is astonishing proof of new hope and life.

COLORS

In this moment of late winter, draw in the rich golds and ruby hues from winter sunsets, so intense in color, and place the magic of the fire inside your home.

Ribbons in these colors should be garlanded everywhere to pep up your psychic energy. Arrange exotic blooms from this color spectrum in your kitchen, and set a permanent place at the table with glass plates or mats and linen in these shades. This is particularly important if you are trying to visualize a relationship with someone moving into the realm of partnership—for the number 2, connected with this second moon of the year, is concerned with pairing and cooperation.

Spread your magic around. Send cards to single friends who would like to feel the stirring of love, and choose an envelope or ribbon to tie around each card in pink-gold hues.

SYMBOLOGY IN MAGIC. Symbols are an ancient part of magic rite and practice, used for their capacity to recall to mind certain predominant aspects of people, relationships, or circumstances. Their use in spell making is an obvious aid to visualization; choosing the right visual metaphor can help you to send very clear messages into the world about yourself or to the person or event you have in mind.

Symbols also play a crucial role in divination, and many oracles employ a simple symbolic system to find the right answer to the querist's questions—the tarot is one manifestation of a symbolic language. What is important is that you feel comfortable with the symbolic language you choose to employ. The symbols are tools of your own psyche—you must direct them!

Having said that, certain symbols have age-old credence in the language of magic, and you could start with some of these and then add symbols that appeal to your own conscious mind.

On the following pages you will find symbols relating to the subjects explored throughout this book and give suggestions for the most easily acquired talismans, or those with the strongest history and mythology.

In all your magic working, choose the symbols that appeal and have the most personal relevance, then combine them with any other instructions given in the master spells to arrive at a signature spell, which should solve any elements of a personal nature you want to incorporate into your magic making.

BEGINNINGS

These symbols are suitable for use in spells to begin a love affair, find a small first house, boost your baby-making potential, inaugurate a business, or start the first day at a new job or educational establishment. The following are useful to wish luck and positivity on any beginnings: SPIDERS initiate the web of vibration: these are very lucky creatures and will bless your beginnings. ACORNS symbolize the tiny beginning from which great and enduring projects may grow. For the Druids, acorns were also connected with immortality. The acorn is perhaps the most powerful single symbol in any magic. The CAMPION flower is a symbol of the first stirrings of love,

or at the very least, some interest! LILAC is also a flower used to symbolize the first love. A BELL signifies the first wish to gain someone's attention. It can be used to make an appeal to be heard—in business or relationships. The NEW MOON is symbolic of a sacred start. The BIRCH tree and birch broom are symbols of the wish to start something properly and see it through.

VISION *and clairvoyance*

The POPPY is a symbol of hypnotic power, dream prophesy, and visions of paradise. PEACOCK FEATHERS are frightening to some witches (my grandmother included) because of their supposed connection with the *"evil eye."* A refusal to be worried by this potent symbol will result in the

power of vision being granted to the querist. The RAINBOW is the arc of communication with the gods—thus, a symbol of inspired communication and vision. Re-creating the rainbow around your house will boost your clairvoyant capacity and ensure good luck. The STAG is a symbol related to clairaudience, because of the stag's sharp sense of hearing. A SPYGLASS signifies the wish to have inside information on an unrevealed situation. The mirror is similar, but is also used for self-revelation. The UNICORN bestows the power to see fairy folk!

LOVE *and feeling*

FLOWERS are the symbol of hope in love. Flora brings the spring flowers, thus awakening love and hopes of joy.

MYRTLE symbolizes fidelity. The SWAN is the bird of Venus; MUSICAL INSTRUMENTS are the messengers of love. The APPLE is the most powerful love talisman, along with the ROSE— the attribute of Venus, and thus of true love. An ARROW kindles love and takes a message sent in thought. A FOUNTAIN symbolizes a garden of love; put one anywhere in your house or garden to draw love to you. CUPIDS have an age-old connection with love. The OAK is the favorite Druidic symbol of lasting love. A CARNATION symbolizes engagement, a KEY a most important love, and a KNOT an indissoluble bond. PEONIES relate to forgiveness in love, and the PANSY is the best flower for love potions and spells!

WORK *and business*
The BEE is a symbol of hard work. CLOVER signifies plenty and good fortune. A THIMBLE means patient work. GOLD RIBBON is symbolic of the bond and commitment to good work with good reward. BRICKS signify solid foundations. An ANT symbolizes work in a community, a SPINNING WHEEL working from home, a LADDER upward ascent and progress in business. COINS are symbolic of gain! The ALDER is the tree of completeness and utility. A SNAIL: working steadily, without rush; SPADE: working with the earth; BIRDS: working toward good of others; SCYTHE or sickle: working with the earth's bounty.

ENCHANTMENT *and passion*
A WILLOW KNOT is a powerful enchanter's tool and symbolic of enchanted, passionate love. HAIR also symbolizes passionate love, and is used to enchant. The CAT is the enchanter's animal, along with the HARE. LILIES (especially tiger lilies) are the flowers of passionate embrace. YARROW is the witch's herb of enchantment and can be used in a love nosegay. A MAGNET is a symbol of powerful attraction, a WEB enchantment, and a CRUCIBLE or CAULDRON the witch's power. THREAD signifies power over fate. A RED ROSE, naturally, represents passion. The PESTLE AND MORTAR are instrumental in empowerment, and are used in making love spells.

DISENCHANTMENT
All of the above, wrapped around with HAWTHORN. CAMPHOR BALLS:

symbols of deterrence; YARROW (herb): used in a way opposite from above, for arresting evil thoughts; a GARLIC BULB: antiseptic, so again, good for refusing bad thoughts from another person; a THORN: slowing progress; a PADLOCK: to refuse access; a "stop" sign!

STRENGTH *and security*
The ACORN (see Beginnings) is a symbol of inner power and determination to become greater. HAIR symbolizes the strength of another in your hands (use wisely). DIAMOND is the hardest and most enduring stone. The number SEVEN is connected with strength: seven sticks are an old symbol of unity, which precludes individual weakness. A HAMMER signifies personal strength and wisdom. The OAK LEAF is a symbol of the tree of strength and wisdom.

ENCIRCLEMENT *or reversal*
A MAGNET; also HOLLY sprigs, measuring COMPASS: designating a new circle; a HAND: normally shown palm upward; in this case, palm down; upside-down TABLE: the tables turned; CLOCK and KEY: symbolic of starting over again with a new cycle; a FIGURE EIGHT; things in a state of flux.

WISDOM *and knowledge*
A BOOK is a symbol of dedication to learning and material as yet unknown. A MAGIC WAND made of hazel is symbolic of ancient knowledge from Mercury. A TREE signifies flourishing; traditionally, this is the apple, sometimes olive, but in Wicca, the

HAZEL. The OWL knows the unknown, nighttime things! CANDLES or a LAMP are symbolic of enlightenment. The SNAIL symbolizes slow degrees of gain and perfection, or patience to learn; a SCROLL or STYLUS: signifies preparedness to listen and learn. The SNAKE is connected with wisdom. A MULBERRY TREE: symbol of prudence.

CELEBRATION *and feasting*
The CORNUCOPIA (horn of plenty). Fruit symbolizes the completed harvest and time to unwind. BRAIDS OF RIBBONS, as in a May dance, signify joyfulness everywhere! The HARP is the celebratory instrument. VINE LEAVES are entwined for celebratory thanks. FLOWERS symbolize the earth's thanks and celebration. GOLD-COVERED AND SILVERED ALMONDS, as used in weddings, symbolize buoyant celebration—and fertility!

RESILIENCE *or survival*
TREES or a forest are symbols of great depth and self-reliance. BLOSSOMS signify that new life is being produced. The HORSESHOE is symbolic in the same way as a magnet but is luckier. A WISHBONE represents ancient luck. GARLIC CLOVES symbolize the ability to fight off any pestilence and ill thought. An IVY LEAF: medical connections and tenacity. The LYRE charms away any threat. The UNICORN (and horn) is a symbol of resilience to all evil. The HEDGEHOG: resilience in general. WINGS (or an angel figure) represent victory over adversity.

HEARTH *and home*
DOLL-SIZED FURNITURE is symbolic of domestic peace; a MODEL HOUSE is similar. SHELLS signify bliss and beauty in the home, a CANDLE HOLDER and FIRE warmth at the center of the house. A BEEHIVE and HONEYCOMB mean a honeyed life in the house. A SPIDER'S WEB: an enchanted realm, made by the persistence of the homemaker; the four elements contained in one space: symbolic of complete riches within the home. THATCHING REED tied around with beautiful ribbon: symbolic of "joy under this roof."

COMPLETION *and finishing tasks*
A WREATH, full circle, RING or measuring COMPASS—all for obvious reasons. A tied-off KNOT: no loose ends. A DOCUMENT TIED IN A PILLOW WITH RIBBON: any paperwork can be used in this way to show you are determined to put it to "bed"; a black DOT: a symbolic period.

TRAVEL *and foreign affairs*
SHELLS, SEAHORSES, SAILS, BOATS, and SAND all symbolize something foreign. GRASSHOPPERS often indicate that someone will travel shortly.

MASTER SPELL: **ASTRAL TRAVEL**. This master spell teaches astral projection, which is a meditative state often helpful to clairvoyant vision. It is also possible literally to "visit" someone and impart an important message, make an apology, or prepare them for some important news or event.

The ingredients of the famous witches' "flying ointments" included hemp, magic mushroom combined with belladonna, and monkshood steeped in tallow. But beware! The herbs that formed the basis of these ointments are dangerous to use, and really must not be handled today—you might become a great witch, but you wouldn't be around for long! For the modern initiate, the heavily drugging herbs that caused hallucination have been replaced by gentler medicines.

YOU WILL NEED
About ²/₃ fl. oz. of almond oil, to which are added 3 drops each of vervain, patchouli, and frankincense; or frankincense, basil, and cinquefoil; or geranium, juniper, and lavender oil; some music; a small glass of white wine (not too cold), steeped with borage flowers or leaves; a large pink-gold candle; a pink-gold ribbon.

MOON PHASE: *Any.*

Set the scene carefully. If you are not comfortable bathing in the mixed oils or massaging a little onto your body, then simply use room fragrances to distribute the scent and induce the hypnotic feeling of these meditative herbs. Sit calmly, breathe in the fragrances, and listen to the music playing very softly. Sip some of the wine very slowly: borage has a very euphoric impact on the senses, so don't hurry the feeling. It is wonderful to do this spell scantily clad, but near a fire. However, modest witches need not worry about this. The most important thing is that you be comfortable, secure, and warm!

Light the candle. Tie the ribbon around your waist and lie back. Imagine the energy spreading from your feet, right through your body, in slow waves, and think of this energy in terms of scent, sound, and warmth drawn from around you. The wine may help to spread the glow! Move the energy very slowly: take at least half a minute to reach your knees, then likewise your hips and chest. Feel the fire spreading, and listen to your breathing. Let your mind float free, as if you were undergoing self-hypnosis. When the warmth, light, and sound have reached your head, imagine yourself free-falling through the universe and feeling utterly safe.

Now, still vaguely aware of the ribbon that anchors you to yourself, drift, and imagine you are angelic, powerful, gentle, and strong, and that you can visit whomsoever you wish. Go slowly: take them a message. In your mind's eye, look them in the eye and tell them anything you want. If you are preparing for a significant event, imagine yourself going through all the motions in a kind of rehearsal.

When you have had enough, imagine you are pulling gently on the ribbon, bringing yourself back to the closer realm of the music, scent, and heat. Wake yourself gently, and as you do, feel your limbs again. Listen to your breathing. Take mental note of anything you learned. You will be able to make wise use of this information.

LOVE

ASH MOON

WATER

IS THE MEDIUM OF FEELING. FOR MANY

PEOPLE, A DEPRESSED STATE CAN BE ALEVIATED SIMPLY

BY PADDLING IN WATER, THEREBY RECHARGING THE EMOTIONAL

BATTERIES. SO PREDOMINANT IS WATER IN OUR COMPOSITION THAT OUR

VERY ESSENCE SEEMS TO BE MADE OF THIS ELEMENT—AND THUS, BY IMPLICATION

(IF THE ANCIENTS KNEW ANYTHING), ARE WE MADE FOR LOVE. THIS CHAPTER

EXPLORES THE REALM OF FEELING. THE COLORS, SCENTS, HERBS, FLOWERS, AND SYMBOLS

THAT RELATE ESPECIALLY TO LOVE ARE EXPLAINED, AND WE DISCOVER HOW TO BUILD AN

INDIVIDUAL SPELL FOR ANY PROBLEM OF THE HEART. AS IN THE PREVIOUS CHAPTER,

HOWEVER, THE INTENTION IS TO SHOW YOU HOW TO MAKE ALTERATIONS TO *any* OF THE

ELEMENTS AND IMPOSE YOUR OWN SIGNATURE ON YOUR MAGIC. WE AGAIN LOOK

CAREFULLY AT RIBBONS AND CORDS, AND AT THE PROPER CHOICE OF CANDLE, AND

PRESENT VARIOUS OPTIONS THAT CAN BE WOVEN INTO EVERYDAY LIFE TO

IMPROVE THE QUALITY AND STRENGTH OF A LOVE BOND WITHOUT ANYONE

ELSE KNOWING THAT THE MAGIC IS BEING WOVEN! NO FESTIVAL

FALLS IN THIS PERIOD, BUT ST. VALENTINE'S DAY

OCCURS JUST BEFORE.

ASH MOON—MOON OF WATERS. Colors: CHERRY-PINK, AMBER. Scent: NEROLI, JASMINE, ROSE ATTAR. Number: 3.

There is some confusion here. In pure numerology, the number 6 governs "pure love," while the number 3 is associated with social life, and very often with the appearance of a third member in the family—i.e. children. However, in the ancient tarot, the number 3 represented the couple with divine guidance, to make the perfect, divine marriage; today, this is seen as the couple and God.

"Mann und Weib und Weib und Mann
Reichen an die Gottheit an."

"Man and wife, and wife and man
Reach toward the divinity."
"THE MAGIC FLUTE"
MOZART's own revisions to Schikaneder's libretto

It is this striving for a perfected union that we are dealing with here, whereas later on in our journey we will address the difficulties that often attend love—such as fear of it, failure in it, and hindrance from others concerning it.

Without question, it is the moon of waters—of *feeling*—that is the moon concerned with love. In line with this, we are aiming at creating, with magical awareness, a union without malice, selfishness, or dominance. The most important step toward this is recognition of the motives that sometimes lead us away from this ideal; and then, too, we must recognize social responsibility within a partnership. A powerful couple of beneficent intention can have an ameliorative impact on those closest to them—not least by example.

So, how is it possible to attain this "divinity"—to continue to delight and surprise and spark the imagination of the one we love, years after the first gloss of a love affair has passed? How can we create a magical relationship, and discover the transfiguring power of a special union with one person who understands us completely, and we them? Is it possible to find, not just our "other half"—for this implies that we are only half a being on our own—but rather, our "extended self"?

The magic of a relationship begins, perhaps, with the recognition that it takes plenty of work, enthusiasm, and imagination to keep it healthy. Our post-Freudian concern with the Self has in some ways led us to expect that a partner must please us, forgetting our reciprocal obligation. We need to address the reality of our own necessary contribution. Equally, of course, we must also stop and assess a relationship with a partner who is doing all the taking—where our own input is out of all proportion and we feel abused. Recognition of these two basic tenets will help you immeasurably in deciding what magic is required: indeed, what is even justified!

There is no specific festival for this period, but you may wish to celebrate Valentine's Day for a week, rather than just one day, to draw out the love festival into greater meaning.

THE RAINBOW OF COLOR IN LOVE MAGIC. And so to the practice of magic in our love lives…. Here, you must draw on a veritable rainbow of colors in order to decide which aspects of love you are trying to appease. Keeping the cherry-pink theme behind all your magic making (or rose-pink if you have lost all hope of ever being happy, or if you have had a lifetime of failures in love), you will find that different aspects of love require different partner colors. In conjunction with the number 3, always choose three colors to work with in love, thereby aspiring to the "divine union."

• If selfishness has been your problem and, bravely, you can recognize this, incorporate the first color, FLAME-RED, into your love magic. This will symbolize the need to go beyond the first principle (you) and reach toward others; that first color will also in some ways represent you; keep it as your signature color until you no longer feel that selfishness is your handicap. This, of course, is equally true for your partner: if the person you love is conditioned to selfish behavior, try using flame-red to symbolize them, and move on to a more sharing color (such as pink-gold) when that ego begins to take a back seat!

• If you are looking to test a relationship's possibilities for moving into real partnership (as opposed to its being perhaps a mere fling), choose PINK-GOLD or RUBY-RED, colors for "pairs." This way, two of the colors in your love spell would be pinks: cherry-pink for love, and pink-gold for partnership.

• If you aspire to marriage itself (the ceremony), the color for marriage and families is INDIGO or BLUE. If your bond is wondrous, but you are trying to find out whether it will ever make it to the altar, two of your colors will be cherry-pink (divine love) and blue or indigo (marriage).

• And the most needed color in love magic? PURPLE, WISTERIA, and LAVENDER are the shades that concern the passions! If you love your partner to bits, but there is simply not enough physical fun, this is your color.

• If you want to overcome the possibility of anything (perhaps the appearance of a potential rival) hindering your happy bond, work magic between you and your love, including the color ROSE-PINK—to which I would add WHITE, for the fulfillment of your wishes and hopes. Three tapers in three shades (choose from those given above) would help to weave gentle, healing thoughts into a worried mind.

• To advance your love affair to higher realms of security, or to share projects of an intellectual nature together—even, perhaps, to strengthen a loving relationship with someone whose intellect and mental powers you respect hugely—the color of strength, security and intellectual analysis is BRICK-BROWN. This would be the right choice for a relationship that has weathered the years with grace and that you want to keep going strong. It would equally be the correct choice for a relationship with a university professor.

• If your lover has hurt you, or you them, and forgiveness is required, burn one CHERRY-colored candle next to an OLIVE or GREEN candle, and perhaps add ROSE-PINK.

• If you have all you need, but wish for a truly enlightened, master association with your "extended self," surround your love with SILVER, WHITE, or GOLD and your love

colors. All these colors respect superior intention.

• If your love relationship is merely waiting for a little cash injection to remove the tensions (or pay for a wedding, or a house, perhaps?), burn a golden, sunshine-YELLOW candle with two others in your chosen love colors to attract material blessings to the union. This might also be your choice if you have fallen for someone who works at the stock exchange or in a bank, or who is obsessed with money to the exclusion of romance. *Do you begin to see how you can play with colors to suit the situation?*

THE SCENT OF LOVE. According to Greek legend, when Venus was born, roses appeared in the world with her. The beautiful and famous Botticelli painting celebrates this, with Zephyr blowing a shower of pink roses from the breeze that wafts Venus to shore.

Subsequently, the rose has become an absolute icon for lovers, and it would be churlish to look farther than this flower for the principal scent for love. What is fascinating is how many times the scent rose attar appears in aromatherapy charts in connection with any uplifting of the senses. We certainly understand better now the connection between the nose and the brain, and the ability of an essential oil to trigger memory, emotion, sexual feelings, learning, and healing—although a *precise* explanation may require many more tests, for many years to come.

For the purposes of magic, it may be enough to say that inhaling rose has a cheering, positive effect on the inhaler. Some cultures have similar relationships with neroli (orange blossom, sacred to marriage in India, for instance) and jasmine (renowned as a love tonic throughout the East and the South Pacific). I would personally add gardenia to this, although it can be difficult to find. Many of these scents have a proven powerful impact on our feelings of passion, as well as of contentment; in any case, few people could be impervious to the delicious fragrances of these wonderful flowers.

In her marvellous "bible" of aromatherapy, *The Fragrant Mind,* Valerie Ann Worwood cites the use of rose in blends for contentment, creativity, happiness, joy, peace, improved performance, and against emotional abuse, among others. In fact, whenever the perfume element has been fundamental to the magic, rose has featured as the key ingredient in love spells for many centuries. So, make this the first scent you buy for love spells of the twenty-first century!

HERBS AND FLOWERS IN LOVE. Herbs are powerful plants. Follow the instructions carefully; if you are pregnant, we recommend extreme caution in the use of herbs of any kind. In fact, if you are sensitive to food products generally, you should seek professional advice before using herbs at any time.

Why and how can herbs affect our emotional state? Will the use of dried lavender, or the addition of fresh pansy flowers to salads, say, make any difference to our happiness in a relationship?

Herbs have weathered thousands of years of climatic change and adapted to a wide range of conditions—adaptations made possible by their complex chemical structure.

Handled properly, these chemicals can in turn help us as individuals to adapt to difficulty and change. This is the basis of herbal medicine—and problems of an emotional or psychological kind are in many ways indivisible from physical problems. There is therefore a genuine physical component to the use of herbs in magic—for they affect us physically.

WILD PANSY (*Viola tricolor*, not the hybrid pansies available from garden centers) relieves pain and promotes healing, cleanses toxins from the system, and is a cordial for the heart. Used (in small doses) in magic spells, it has a positive effect on our physical and psycho-emotional states. Symbolically, it represents the one we have "thoughts" of—hence "pansy," from the French *pensées*, meaning thoughts.

The VIOLET is closely related to the pansy, and is another herb perennially appealing in love magic. Now believed to be beneficial in anti-cancer treatment, violet combats exhaustion and nervous skin conditions, has a pleasant taste in wine and candy, and was incorporated in love potions and massage creams. Again, the flowers can be used in salads, and may have a tonic effect, leading to a loving feeling.

VERVAIN (verbena) is used for love philters and as the basis of love potpourris. This herb is excellent for nervous complaints, which might explain its benefit in emotional terms—a relaxed soul is always more attractive to a potential admirer! Vervain also stimulates the uterus, making women feel quite sensual. *But do not use during pregnancy.*

BORAGE has a reputation for lifting the spirits and inducing a natural euphoria. Wine made from borage (or steeped with it) has long been held to "make men and women glad and merry" (John Gerard, *The Herball*, 1597); it has been recommended as an addition to salads and also gives a certain *je ne sais quoi* to cakes and teas, in terms of both the flavor and the spiritual! At the very least, modern herbalists attribute antidepressant properties to the herb.

YARROW (milfoil) is the age-old divinatory herb, used in the regime accompanying questions to the Chinese oracle the *I Ching*. It is a relaxant and can lower blood pressure; also has a history of use for menstrual complaints. Add it to potpourris, especially for the bedroom.

ALCHEMILLA (lady's mantle) is the "little magic" herb, known for its alchemical connection. It can also be used in a variety of ways to treat female disorders, primarily heavy periods. It symbolizes the woman in love, and water collected from within its leaves is powerful in magic.

ARTEMESIAS are many and varied. They are too poisonous to use internally, and should always be handled with care. Grow a little southernwood (*Artemisia abrotanum*)

in the garden to attract "lad's love." Another artemisia, wormwood, was the basis for absinthe and vermouth, but its use is now restricted.

PERIWINKLE (*Vinca*) is another herb connected with the control of female problems. It is known to reduce blood pressure, and was called "sorcerer's violet" in reference to its power in love potions.

LADY'S BEDSTRAW (*Galium verum*) was made into an ointment with tallow, said to be a great relief for the aching limbs of weary travelers. The herb was also strewn for its odorous effects on lifting the spirits in the bedchamber!

LOVAGE is superb added to salads or sprinkled on fresh soups and tomatoes. In love, it is pleasant to inhale the aroma, which has an invigorating effect, and it also aids relaxation—but use just a little.

POPPIES are a dangerous subject! The field poppy is the only poppy that can be used legally, and the seeds are safe to add to cooking, where they have a very uplifting effect. This poppy is also connected with pain relief in a less traumatic way than its relative, the opium poppy, which is addictive. For cooking, you should use only the seeds you can buy commercially. If you grow the corn poppy, use the red petals in potpourris.

BASIL is the most seductive of all Mediterranean herbs, cheering the spirit with its spicy aroma and calming the nerves when ingested. It is the most romantic herb for Italians, for whom it symbolizes deep love. Growing the plant is thought to be lucky, and nurturing it from seed is a signal to the divine spirit that you are ready for love.

The leaves of MYRTLE are used to flavor pork dishes and lamb. The connection with love is age-old and may be the result of its capacity to sweeten the breath.

MEADOWSWEET, sacred to the Druids, was used to flavor wines and to strew in the most important rooms: Gerard tells us it "makes the heart merrier." Use it in the bath to put your partner (and yourself, if the bathtub is big enough for two) in a loving mood.

CILANTRO, OR CORIANDER, is an aromatic stimulant, and was added to love potions because of its aphrodisiac properties.

DIANTHUS (clove carnation) is a favorite ingredient in love potions and potpourris. This wonderful herb has a myriad uses: add the flowers to salads, wine, and cakes, and use in sauces, vinegars, and ales. It sweetens the breath, banishes headaches, quenches thirst, and brings on a gentle sweat. Need I say more?

With LAVENDER, we have saved the best till last. What does this herb not do? It is renowned in love for its capacity to alleviate nervous tension, ease digestive problems, and tranquilize after an overstimulating day. It also cheers the mind and kills bacteria and was added to soaps and baths for its obvious user-friendly properties. Indeed, for its antibacterial action alone it would be a friend to lovers. As an essential oil, it makes a wonderful salve for weary limbs, and can help ease skin disorders. Use it in cooking to rally flagging spirits!

USING THE MAGIC OF LOVE. You now have some of the tools with which to build a loving house. You should incorporate color, scent, herbs, and symbols wherever they please you. Choose those you like, that you can obtain readily, that are within your budget, and that perhaps have a certain significance for the love problem you want to solve.

The master spell in this chapter will provide you with the basic elements of a spell to attract (or strengthen) a love tie; if you want to get over a love relationship, see pages 88-107 instead.

Remember that you can choose whichever elements are relevant to *you*. Among the symbols presented on pages 37-39, you should be able to find something pertinent to *your* lover, and the same is true for scents and herbs.

THERE ARE NO ABSOLUTES IN SPELL MAKING—save for the warning not to become entangled with magic that is in any way detrimental to another being. Therefore, feel free to be creative.

DESIGN A SPELL YOU LIKE THE LOOK, FEEL, AND SMELL OF—AND MAKE IT YOUR OWN.

MASTER SPELL: **TO ATTRACT LOVE.** This spell will work, with minor amendments, for a love who is as yet unknown, or for someone you are attracted to with (so far) no result, or for a person who has been flirting and playing with your feelings without becoming more serious.

YOU WILL NEED

1 yard of cherry-pink ribbon, and 2 other colors (see choices on page 45); a flask of red wine, to which are added flowering herbs of your choice (pansy, borage, and dianthus are good for this, but use what you like); a dish of water to symbolize emotion; a cherry-pink taper, and 2 others (as before); clouds of incense burning to focus your thoughts (again, choose your favorite: benzoin or frankincense would be the usual choice, but you may prefer an essential oil simmering in a fragrancer); a lock of your hair.

MOON PHASE: *Full. Traditionally, this spell would be apt for Valentine's Day or the Spring Solstice—both of which occur near the time of the ash moon.*

Braid the three ribbons together, and tie them around your brow or waist. Strain your wine and sip a little in toast to the new era of love you are about to embark upon. Gaze up to the moon and ask a blessing of love; for the moon rules the realm of dreams. Ask that your dreams be transposed to the realm of earth—and stamp your foot softly on the ground to symbolize this. If you have anyone in particular in mind, say their name.

Say to the moon and starlight, *"Lovely lady's light that illumines the land, Seek out and bring my lover to hand, I offer my heart full of candor and pleasure, That soon may our lives meet in work or in leisure."* Meditate on the love you want.

Remember that the clearer and brighter your visualization, the more powerful your magic. Be sure you are not aiming your thoughts at someone who is tied to another.

Place the dish of water in a position where it can reflect the light—either from the candles you will light in a moment or from the moon. Now, turning to your candles and your incense or oil burner, light them with the words *"Love lights the way"* each time. If there is someone you are trying to entice, follow the phrase with their name as you light the candles.

Place the lock of hair in the center of the space created by the candles. Send the beam of candlelight into the air, higher and higher, until you can see it form a heart shape above you. Imagine the sound of laughter from your (known or unknown) lover. Breathe in the scent, and pass your lock of hair through it. Keep this for later, and place it beside your bed.

The spell is complete when you feel you have sent your thought with sufficient strength. You can then untie the ribbon, and put it playfully in any number of spaces in your life: on your steering wheel, around your front-door knob, at your mailbox, in your underwear drawer, in your purse, around your dog's neck, even around your own! It would be nice tied around your pillow—to bring truth to your dreams.

After your tapers have burned down a little, extinguish them, and reserve them for that special dinner you expect to share with your loved one.

SPRING

WE

HAVE COME THROUGH THE WINTER

MOONS, AND COULD NOW TURN OUR THOUGHTS

TO THE SEASON OF SPRING IN ITS OWN RIGHT.

EACH SEASON HAS ITS GENTLE TASKS AND RHYTHMS TO BE

PERFORMED. IN SPRING, WE ARE INSPIRED BY THE REBIRTH OF

THE EARTH; NATURE IS STIRRING, AND THE FORCE FIELDS OF

THE EARTH ARE NO LONGER APPARENTLY DORMANT. MAGIC WORKED AT

THIS TIME SHOULD DRAW ON THE EXTRAORDINARY PUSH FOR LIFE

AND MOVEMENT THAT CAN BE FELT AFTER MONTHS OF NO ACTIVITY.

THE WITCH NOW TURNS HER ATTENTION TO MATTERS SUCH AS PERSONAL SPRING

CLEANING, AS WELL AS THE PRACTICAL TASKS OF SOWING HERBS AND

FLOWERS THAT SHE WILL USE IN MAGIC AND HEALING

THROUGHOUT THE YEAR. AND, MOST IMPORTANTLY, IF YOU

TUNE INTO THE MARVELOUS SPRING FEELING OF BEING

ALIVE AGAIN, MAGICAL THINGS WILL BE DRAWN TO YOU

IN ALL SPHERES OF YOUR LIFE. ELEMENT: AIR.

DIRECTION: EAST.

The Spring Equinox. This is usually March 21st in the northern hemisphere and September 21st in the southern, though it may vary by a day or so because of leap years. At this moment, as the name suggests, the earth is in perfect balance and day and night are of equal length.

This was a powerful festival in times gone by. The sun—which was considered to be male—was in perfect harmony with the moon—which was female; the solstice is a divine symbol for the female receptivity of the earth preparing to take the (male) seed, and blossom forth. The first signs of spring flowers bursting with life are evidence that all is right in the divine world and that the earth is blessed.

This month (approximately corresponding to our April) was given the Anglo-Saxon name of the goddess Oestra (or Eostre—Ostara in Latin); the corruption of this to Easter is self-evident. Certainly, the festival celebrates the return of the goddess from winter and the burgeoning of spring with the promise of work ahead.

It is even probable that the hot cross bun of the Easter feast is derived from the female circle intersected by the male cross—the Celtic cross. The Easter rabbit also stems from Pagan mythology, which recalls a rabbit or hare, messenger of the moon, honoring the goddess with a gift of the precious eggs that symbolized life by laying them at her feet, covered in a rainbow of colors. We re-enact the drama still.

Painting eggs, strewing rainbows of flowers, baking buns or breads and marking them with a cross, and especially growing hyacinths (which resemble wild bluebells) for your altar or table are ways of honoring the old magic within a modern context. Easter wine infused with a pinch of saffron and some blue flowers (try borage or violet) will put you in a wonderful loving mood—and honor the need for sowing the seeds of your future as well!

Any work is achieved better through proper preparation. Flowers grow better when the rank weeds are removed and the hard-packed soil is combed and raked to a fine tilth. So it is with life. Magic can put us in the right frame of mind to undertake a task with dignity, stamina, and strength, while also adding a spark of playfulness to what might have been a dull chore. Add magical touches to all your workings, and watch the hours disappear more quickly while—magically—the successful outcome of your endeavor is also more assured.

To weave magic into your work requires a little creative thought. Performing magic spells in relation to work and gain will not bypass the need for your own contribution: it is not a formula for avoiding work and expecting the universe to provide. Instead, all the little rituals you introduce into your business life will be asking that work continue to find you—that you have plenty to do. An honest heart performing these rites will be hoping for ongoing opportunities, and luck in finding happy circumstances in a fulfilling working life.

THE HEARTBEAT OF SPRING. This is the Season of Oestra, Goddess of Light and Fertility. Nature imbues us with teeming life; all creatures are brimming with sexual appetite and peak fecundity. From Oestra springs the festival of Ostara, renamed Easter by the Church. We still celebrate the potency of the egg as the symbol of renewal and the image of life waiting to burst forth—you will recognize this connection in the word "estrogen."

This is the magical moment for spring cleaning. Just as the trees begin to blossom, so may we. Our minds should be energized and our health and beauty flushed with optimism and vitality. Kick out all outworn premises, and start from fresh anywhere your life seems jaded.

It is time to use the besom, or witch's broom, for rebirth. This is a symbolic act, but whipping up energy from this amazing symbol of fertility will really give you a buzz. Either make a broom yourself from birch twigs or strong herbs like rosemary, or ask a friend to give you one for luck; otherwise, you can use an ordinary household broom. Sweep through your home from front door to back, then out the front again, to rid you and your home from any doubts, anxieties, and lack of confidence. When you have finished, face the east, direction of spring and the rising sun, and invite in a whole new determination and positivity. Put wind chimes or a hanging bell in the east to welcome spring and hear her voice. Place a carefully chosen stone, such as a gem or crystal, in an eastern corner of your house or garden: this will draw and radiate magic from the east. This is the first and most important act of the new spring.

Traditionally, this is the time to plan and lay out a new garden and, in particular, a healing garden, for these are the energies of spring. If you are short of space, try to devote a kitchen window box to some of the following healing herbs: peppermint, sage, carnation, garlic, onion or chives, rue, lavender, marjoram, or sorrel. Sow the seeds yourself if you want them to be especially magical. Your love and energy feed the seedlings with an extra dimension of love, and thus magic. Any spells you wish to do that involve planting little herbs or shrubs should be done now. An excellent example is the one on the following page.

A RITE OF SPRING: STEPPING FROM OLD INTO NEW. "NEW LIFE IN AN OLD SHOE, I'LL BE MERRY WHATEVER I DO." Boots and shoes are an ancient symbol of prosperity and longevity. If boots were lost or toppled over, a miner might prefer not to work in the mines that day or a seaman not set sail for work. The idea of "filling someone's shoes" is still used as a mark of having a long way to go to live up to another person's high qualities. As a ritual to welcome in the earliest days of spring, try this sowing of spring dreams.

YOU WILL NEED
Packets of mixed flower and/or herb seeds; an old pair of garden boots or clogs; soil; plastic film.

Choose wonderful flowers for this exercise, which is designed to have all your hopes germinate along with the seedlings after the chilly days of winter have past. Traditional seeds include love-in-a-mist (*Nigella damascena*), lad's love (*Artemesia*), kiss-me-in-the-buttery (pansy), maiden pink (dianthus), or summer savory (*Satureja hortensis*), whose names reveal their potency for love potions and pouches. The very last, summer savory, sown in spring and sprouting in June and July, is a favorite old aphrodisiac—sometimes called the "herb of happiness"—and well worth growing.

Pack the boots with good soil, then sow the seeds lightly on top of the soil and sprinkle a fine tilth over them. Water gently, speaking your dreams of new projects (in keeping with the nature of spring) over them. Cover them gently with film, and place them somewhere light and protected, where you can tend them with love.

Thin out the seedlings toward the middle of spring, but let a few of each continue to grow in the boots, where they can flower directly. As the first seedling appears, make a wish and blow it to the east. As the first flower appears, pluck it with a wish and bring it indoors to a special altar, then press it in a personal book, locket, or diary.

Watch your dreams grow into truths.

OSTARA EGGS. One beautiful Ostara custom is that of painting and decorating eggs, which symbolize the life force. A willow basket of eggs is a traditional omen of luck and strength, and can be incorporated into your magic making.

Use hard-boiled eggs, which can also be symbolically returned to the earth as part of a ritual. Choose wonderful colors to write, in tiny writing, little wishes and love spells on your eggs. Use pink to draw related images and write sweet words concerning a loved one. If you seek greater balance in a relationship, try drawing the scales, or the Yin and Yang symbol (see page 147). These images for peace in love are in keeping with the energies of spring balance, especially at the equinox.

On other eggs you could paint backgrounds in appropriate colors: pink for love, blue for loyalty and stability, yellow for intellectual spark, red for passion, mauve for psychic activity, silver for feminine beauty, gold for money, and green for health. Superimpose symbols of joy that are personal to you and those you love, perhaps hearts, letters, rings, flowers, or clouds.

Be creative, and make up your own messages. Place the decorated eggs in a beautiful basket on an altar from late March through early April, the first couple of weeks of the sign of Aries, symbolizing action.

For a really special spell, you can "blow" an egg. Make little holes carefully in each end of the egg, then blow out the contents very gently. Dip the egg carefully in glue and glitter, then decorate it with braids, threads, or ribbons, using the same colors given above to determine the area of spell. If you are very nimble-fingered, you may be able to make a hole at one end just big enough for you to feed a tight scroll of rice paper into it.

First write on the paper a spell with an incantation of love dedicated to the one you love. Do this in your own words, asking for the energy of spring to imbue new passion and power into a love affair. This would work particularly well on a not-very-physical relationship into which you would like to encourage more sensuality.

Using a very long needle, thread a little piece of thread or ribbon through your decorated egg to tie it to a branch of a budding tree. Tie a knot in the bottom of the ribbon, perhaps with a bead or button attached, then hang the egg from the top. As you hang your egg spell face the east and ask the maiden to bless your endeavors, wishes, and hopes with her most beguiling energies and powers of persuasion.

SPRING LOVE INCENSE. The theory of incense in ritual is that it carries thought through the astral plane, converting ideas into a more tangible essence. It also helps to stimulate intellectual and mental energy, sharpening our focus of thought for a while. We can both clear our heads of debris and open up a dialogue with the magical ether.

YOU WILL NEED

1/2 teaspoon each ground cinnamon and cloves; 1 teaspoon powdered frankincense; a pinch of nutmeg; 1 teaspoon powdered dry myrtle or vervain leaves (the latter can be found as a tea at health food stores and ground down in a mortar and pestle).

A commercial blend of incense will give joyous results; however, even more pleasure will be derived from making your own blend, controlling the elements you wish to awaken into thought, such as love, sensuality, positivity, or success. Spring is the best time to make incense, partly because the senses are stirring, but also because spring rules the element of air, through which smoke must pass. Summer is also a good season, because of its association with fire.

I find a mortar and pestle is the easiest piece of equipment to use for blending incense, though I know some people much prefer a blender. Practice with both, and see what works best for you. Gum resins such as benzoin or frankincense add cohesion to the other elements in incense and are easiest to work when they are cool, then ground with the other ingredients.

Work the ingredients together well. Depending on the temperature, you will get a gummy pellet or a more powdered lump that can be rolled into a pellet by dusting it with more sticky frankincense powder. To burn your incense you will need a charcoal burner, which can be found at most stores where you buy incense.

Put the burner on a heatproof surface, such as a strong ceramic dish or metal container, or on the stone hearth of a fireplace. Place the incense on the burner and light. Face again to the east, waft the smoke in that direction, and offer up very simply worded (and unselfish) prayers concerning your desire for love. Breathe in the scent for about 15 minutes, then let the smoke drift around your home to draw love to your dwelling place.

Sprinkle any ashes that are left over on budding plants, asking once more for a new budding love and for joy in your personal life. As soon as you have performed this incense ritual, understand that the love vibration has begun somewhere in the astral for you. Leave it with good feelings, and do not emit any panic or anxiety as to what will happen next. Just exude a gentle confidence that life has just begun anew. Keep spring flowers (even the smallest nosegay) in your home as you prepare for this love.

ROSE-COLORED DREAMS. To dream a prophetic and inspiring dream of enchantment that will excite the feelings of a loved one for you.

YOU WILL NEED

1 tablespoon fresh rose petals, or dried apothecary's rose;
1 teaspoon jasmine petals, or jasmine tea (but fresh flowers are best);
1 vanilla pod; 1 stick cinnamon; 1 teaspoon fresh or dried vervain;
a pink china cup; 1 rose-scented candle; 1 drop benzoin oil in
1 teaspoon carrier oil; 1 yard rose-pink satin ribbon.

Make a brew of this delicious concoction before retiring to bed. Combine the first five ingredients and pour boiling water over. Allow to brew for about ten minutes, then strain into a pretty cup. Before you sip, light the candle, massage your temples very gently with the oil, and tie the ribbon loosely around your waist. Sip, and think beautiful, romantic thoughts. The more strongly you can visualize, the more effective will be the spell.

SHOWER WITH ROSES. Here is a beautiful purification ritual for self-initiation, designed to deepen understanding and sharpen focus on the world around you.

Under the magic of this moment, with the balance equal between the moon's influence over emotion and feeling, and her receptive powers, and the sun's influence over our active, physical persona and our conscious being, the witch embarks on a magical journey. Now is the time to step forward into initiation.

Ceremonial bathing marks a departure from an outworn perception and the move to a new one. A shower has the feeling of spring about it, so you can make this a quick but profound personal statement. If you prefer the unhurried ritual of a bath, you can add in elements of personal significance.

In your bathroom, create a circle of light made by five points, usually candles, loosely in a star shape. Use either a commercial rose shower gel, or make one of your own using baby shampoo and a few drops of rose oil. Take one real rose, and after you've showered, but before drying, stroke the rose over your body, symbolizing a new heightened awareness, a dedication to love and nature, and a declaration of innocence. Address the goddess and the god in your own words, expressing your

intention to lead a magical life, asking for their blessings and guidance. Let your body air-dry as much as possible before you dress and step out of the circle of light.

Now witness the death of the non-witch before you. Find an old photo of you that you no longer like, or which was perhaps taken at an unhappy moment. Cover it in black paper or cloth, and consign it either to the attic or to the bin! Now you can assume a new name, which might be a nickname, or a middle name, or something completely new.

Create a permanent corner that will be your altar, perhaps in the garden with some special stones. Address this with the witches' chant: "*I, (your new name), walk the path of the world now as a witch (or Wiccan, if you prefer)." Celebrate your new birthday with cakes and ale, consumed in a circle of rose-scented candles, sharing the bounty. Promise yourself never to do the bidding of anyone, only to follow the rule to harm none and work only good magic.

CONJURING SALT. Salt is a precious and powerful commodity, used in witchcraft to protect and consecrate the area in which you work, such as a circle. Control of the salt is also essential for survival and strength. Legend says that King Arthur's table was round so that every knight would be the same distance from the salt, the closer to the salt, the more favor and power one had.

A dish of salt or salt sprinkled into a circle of protection will bring the magic force into line with the elements of creation. Salt imbues the consumer with powerful sight and knowledge; it is also said that salt shared between friends helps to achieve likeness of mind.

Perform the ritual of the salt as near to the Spring Equinox as possible, perhaps with some friends, as a preface to working magic from spring onward. On a sunny day, go somewhere close to running water—a river or stream, or the seashore. You could dedicate the salt to Diana, if you feel comfortable with that.

As near as you can manage to noon, take a handful of rock or sea salt and go to the water's edge; kneel beside it and say: *"I conjure thee, great salt, to rest here in the stream of life and here at noon-tide; I cast my eyes to the sun and back to the water once more, that I may know my future, to prepare for what must be, and that I may gain control of all the irritations of my life that distract me from my path of mental calm and enlightenment. Beside the rising stream I take my place, and see the water around. And likewise I think on the growing sun, and in the water, sun and salt my soul finds strength, and asks the answers of great mysteries. Blessed be."*

Now cast the salt, all but a tiny pinch, out into the water as an offering to nature and to Diana. Ask that you be given powers of discernment and wisdom, and that you may use these powers for the betterment of those around you and as unselfishly as possible. Finally, taste the remaining morsel of salt and consume it as a vow to careful thought, hard work, and generous action. Bow a last time to these elements and say: *"Water, sun, and salt, be gracious unto me."*

You are now empowered as a human being and ready to work good spells from spring through summer and fall, before a period of relative quiet around the "wheel of the year" (at Yule). "Pinch" some salt and taste it before every important occasion.

WORK

ALDER MOON

THE

ALDER MOON RUNS FROM MID-MARCH TO

EARLY APRIL. HERE, WE BEGIN TO LOOK AT THE YEAR'S

WORK AND AT HOW TO EXECUTE OUR OWN DUTIES EFFECTIVELY AND

ENJOYABLY. THIS MOON GOVERNS ROUTINE BUSINESS AND HARD WORK, AS

OPPOSED TO THE LAUNCH OF ANYTHING REALLY SPECTACULAR, AND SPELLS

PERFORMED UNDER ITS SWAY WILL ENSURE A FAIR RESULT FROM THE ENTERPRISE. WE

ADDRESS THE ASPECT OF MAGIC IN PREPARATION FOR ALL KEY THINGS: DIGGING THE

SOIL IN READINESS FOR SOWING SEEDS, PLANNING FOR SUCCESS IN OUR WORKING LIFE AND

STUDY, KEEPING A ROBUST BUSINESS THRIVING! THE MASTER SPELL IS FOR BRINGING

HAPPINESS AT WORK, FOR WORK DONE CHEERFULLY ALWAYS HAS BETTER RESULTS, AND WE

DISCOVER HOW TO OVERCOME PROBLEMS AT WORK. THE ALDER MOON REMINDS US THAT

NOTHING IS GAINED WITHOUT SOME COMMITMENT AND PERSEVERANCE, AND THIS IS

REFLECTED IN THE TWO SYMBOLS FOR THIS CHAPTER. ONE IS "PATIENCE": THE

TORTOISE, OR THE SNAIL, BOTH LONG-HELD TALISMANS OF PATIENT WORK

AND STEADY PROGRESS. THE OTHER IS THE "GARDEN"—WHERE

WHAT IS USEFUL MAY ALSO BE BEAUTIFUL. PREPARE

YOUR GROUND, AND BLOSSOM FORTH!

ALDER MOON—MOON OF UTILITY AND SELF-GOVERNANCE. Colors: INDIGO, DEEP BLUE. Scents: CITRUS, BERGAMOT. Number: 4. The soundest preparation for success in any venture is to approach it with a determined, practical, and independent spirit. Magic views work as vital to the process of life: only after hard work is completed is a celebration felt in the very soles of the feet!

THE COLORS OF WORK

An environment of blues will help you to think, study, and concentrate. Indigo is a powerful color for business, and of course blue is a primary color, just as work—be it mental or physical—is requisite to life. These colors embody the magic combination of clarity and stimulation, plus a reduction of tension. In other words, surrounding yourself with blues while you work will help you to focus your mind and find inner energy, and will neither sap your strength nor distract or stress you. Any office should have a strong blue element if it is to support the mental activity of the people who work therein. If painting the walls seems too radical, place a blue cushion on your chair, or hang a bluish picture near your desk. Or wear blue clothes on a day when you simply have to get a lot done.

Then, naturally, there are the magic things to do: tie a blue ribbon around your computer when you close it down at night, so that it is there to greet you first thing the next day. Place a blue candle on your desk, and light it when you feel weary. Buy a blue coffee mug in a shade that inspires, and when you take a break, "breathe in" the color of the cup. If you really

feel uninspired by the work you have to get through in order to meet a deadline, blue flowers in a vase—or, better still, a blue-flowered potted plant growing on your windowsill or desk—will really help to recharge your batteries at the moments of greatest apathy. And of course, you'll laugh when you think of it—especially if your boss has no idea why you have surrounded the latest project with potted blue hyacinths or African violets! Blue plates on the table, blue curtains, even a blue folder, will all help you get the job done more calmly.

THE SCENTS OF WORK

The citrus scents of orange, lemon, and grapefruit, plus bergamot, all have a purposeful effect on the mind and creative imagination. These oils are associated with energy, confidence, and positive performance, dispelling apathy and confusion, and piquing the brain into action. Perhaps for this reason, shower gels are now often spiked with citrus smells to get us going in the morning, and even men's grooming products favor bergamot to add a bracing quality to the unfolding day. Incorporating these fragrances into our work routine will make it easier to deal with the demands placed on us in a stressful society.

ORANGE may be the most important individual choice: neroli (orange blossom) is equally good here. If overwork and mental strain are a problem, this scent will neutralize the bad feelings that accompany such conditions.

LEMON is an antidote to feelings of sluggishness and tiredness, which are a common problem in work of every kind—even if you normally enjoy what you do.

GRAPEFRUIT helps to overcome frustrations (which might be caused by difficult relationships with others at work, or perhaps a job that never quite seems to get finished!) and can be useful if you are feeling apprehensive or indecisive. Adding a touch of

GINGER, **BASIL**, or **ROSEMARY** will help to counteract forgetfulness. Perhaps your work demands that you keep a thousand little things in your mind all the time—and in fact, these three scents are excellent in companionship with the other oils above if you have to study for an exam or absorb difficult schoolwork.

Assess the problems at the core of your working life, then choose any two or three of these oils to add to your blue colors, and push yourself back into peak performance. There is nothing wrong with burning these oils on your desk, or infusing your blue candle and lighting it for a few minutes several times a day. If others around you complain of the smell, keep a little blue herb pillow in your desk, sprinkle it with oil, and then inhale privately. You may set some tongues wagging—or you could set a trend!

PROBLEMS AT WORK

Sometimes, no matter how tolerant you try to be, someone just puts you on edge and makes you feel threatened. Maybe the person is more dominant than you, or seems to have a better relationship with someone in authority. The reverse is equally possible—that you have somehow engendered the wrath and jealousy of another! If you have to work with this person on a regular basis, you must deal with the difficulty or run the risk of making your job intolerable.

Jealousy and personality discord account for a huge amount of work misery, and sometimes result in a stand-off where one or the other of the parties feels compelled to resign. Don't let this happen, when there are witchy cures for the problem. What you must recognize, though, is that you do not want to make the other person more hostile (so revenge spells are definitely out!); you need, instead, to make them like you much better, until all animosity has been banished.

Bring a blue-flowered potted plant into the work domain, write both your name and that of your "adversary" on one small piece of paper, and push this gently into the soil around the plant. Tie the pot itself with ribbons—blue for perfected work, and either sunshine yellow (symbolizing a reversal of current circumstances) or olive green (symbolic of forgiveness). Place the plant somewhere everyone can enjoy it, and nurture it. Each time you water it, say something nice about the other person. Soon you will have them purring more contentedly around you!

DRESSING FOR INTERVIEWS

Whatever fashion magazines dictate, a witch's advice for job interviews will always start with the wearing of blue underwear! My husband wears blue silk boxer shorts for important work occasions—and no one (I suppose) knows about this but me, but it gives him focus and self-discipline from the ground up!

With this as the starting point, individual taste will determine whether the outfit itself should be smart or casual, a skirt or pants, velveteen or linen. Try to arrange the meeting for a new moon, and begin by bathing (or showering) with those citrus scents. Don't wear any designer fragrance, but do put on some of the diluted citrus oils, or dab a little undiluted onto your watch strap, purse, belt, or briefcase—the person talking to you will be just as alert as you!

When you get home, give a libation (a small drink) of ale or wine to your favorite tree in the park or in your yard. Traditionally, this would have been an alder tree, but any tree will suffice as long as you explain that you are hoping for strong growth to come from the seed you have just planted at your interview. This has always been lucky for those I know.

STARTING A BUSINESS

If you are trying to launch a concern of your own—be it a sandwich shop, a design business, a career as a pop star, a caregiving agency, or perhaps a career as a writer—till the soil first! Wait for a new moon before "going public" or signing any contracts; choose a name that has the letter "d," "m," or "v" in it to signify an inclination to work hard—a letter for material success ("h," "q," or "z") will also be a huge help.

The next step is to get your color scheme right: remember to put blue somewhere to the fore, and couple this with any color that symbolizes the kind of work you do (see notes on color in each moon chapter). Tie ribbons and balloons everywhere to get attention and put energy into the new operation; regularly burn candles infused with the scents described on page 69 in the window or near the phone. And definitely put plants of glowing good health all around you—especially those with blue flowers.

Last, write the name of your new business on a small piece of paper, and on the full moon after you have launched, take it to some running water. Let it go with the blessing that your new working life will be like a river of depth, feeling, gentle power, and the ability to adapt to any circumstances, and watch it sail forth into the world. Be confident, and you will not fail.

KICK-STARTING A SLUGGISH BUSINESS

The first cure for a business (yours or anyone else's) that is making slow progress is to inject energy into it everywhere. This is a fun project, and you should draw everyone into it!

Write the name of the suffering business on paper and place it under a red candle (for a new start) and a blue candle, either in the office or in your home. Tie a white ribbon around the base of each one, to add more power via white light. Burn the candles for an hour or two each day, and imagine light moving around the business environment, gaining energy and attracting interest from lots of people. Put a potted plant (blue, of course!) in a prominent spot in the workplace, and push the name that has been under your candles into the soil. Tie the ribbon around the plant. Meanwhile, tie a red ribbon around the telephone at work: this encourages more calls. Sprinkle a few drops of citrus oil near the threshold of the workplace, to put visitors in a zappy, responsive state of mind. Mark the place in the telephone book where the office number appears with a card dotted with a little of the oil, and put a blue ribbon in there, too.

Finally, send thriving plants (oddly enough, potted cilantro tied with blue ribbon is a good choice here) all over the place to attract more activity into the business: give them to friends and family, and offer them to acquaintances. Distributing growing plants in this way will send out signals of "good grace" concerning the business.

CONTINUED SUCCESS

If yours is the happy predicament of being really fortunate and fulfilled in your choice and situation of work, and you merely wish to keep it that way ad infinitum, yours is the simplest magic to perform, but you will nevertheless be pleased with the result. Many people take success for granted—as their right—and forget to show grace when they are favored.

Take a silver coin and place it in the palm of your hand, facing the sunlight, so that it glints a little in the light. Say thanks many times over for the flow of work and funds that has come your way, then say the name of your business or the place where you work, four times out loud. Wrap the coin in blue cloth or ribbon, and place it somewhere over the door in your office, or tape it to the desk at which you work. Touch it every so often with a brief word of thanks.

HONORS AT SCHOOL OR COLLEGE

Absorb every bit of the advice given so far in this chapter in one way or another into your life as a student. Put a potted plant with beautiful blue flowers on your new teacher's desk each year; cover boring textbooks with indigo (and silver) paper; keep a ribbon impregnated with the citrus scents in your pencil case, and breathe it in whenever you are having a humdrum day; and try to present really important work in a blue-bordered folder.

Before your first day at a new institution, plant a seedling of a blue, fragrant flower (sweet peas are always my favorite), and write your own name and that of the new college teacher, or whatever, on a piece of paper pushed gently into the pot. On really dull days (weather- or subject-wise), ask your teacher or professor if you can hang a balloon, place a vase of flowers, or scent the room with a burner to keep everyone attentive: they probably won't mind a bit. My daughter has a bookmark saturated with lime and lemon which she places in her math books when required: this is her least favorite subject, and the scents help her to knuckle down to the work at hand.

Although much work is arduous duty, it is always completed more quickly and satisfactorily if you bring a sparkle to it. I first fell in love with Schubert's *"Death and the Maiden"* while I was scrubbing my kitchen floor—for it literally transported me above the humdrum task. Forever after, scrubbing the floor has been the moment to discover new music, and lose myself in the task.

DOMESTIC WORK

Never let it be thought that bringing up a family is unrecognized by this witch for the truly hard work that it is. I think raising a family and managing a home (of whatever size) well is the hardest job of all—especially if it is combined with part-time work, study, or community responsibility. There is a special magic to help temper the demands of a busy home—and again, it should also put a little more fun into routine work.

Think over the daily run of chores, and decide what objects can receive the playful blue ribbon or the drops of oil. Visitors to my house will often see ribbons tied to refrigerator doors, irons, bottles of dishwashing detergent, washing baskets, and brooms. All these make me laugh when I have to settle down to the job required with each item. There is also a huge blue ribbon tied to the chair I sit on when writing. Without this I might experience energy block—especially when I have essays, letters, chapters of books, and a baby vying for my time. Think blue ribbons everywhere!

The next step is to decorate the windowsill of the room in which you work most with plants that will thrive in that environment. My desk boasts a potted lemon tree—combining two ideas, as it were—and basil, cilantro, and African violets jostle together on the windowsill. I also have a blue hydrangea on the windowsill in my bedroom—which is where I often read, study, and perform magic.

Lastly, the element that governs work is "earth"—so work with some as often as you can. Plant a seedling every so often, or cultivate a window box, if a full garden is out of the question. Quite simply, dirtying your hands is good for all business!

MASTER SPELL: **FOR HAPPINESS IN WORK.** This spell is based on the simple concept that the happier we are in what we do, the more successful we will be at it. It also safeguards contentment in all the aspects of our work: socially, financially, and in terms of challenge. You will not be taken for granted by anyone.

YOU WILL NEED

1 yard each of blue and gold cord, of the same texture; a piece of paper; an emblem of your work; golden yellow sunflowers (symbolizing both material success and happiness of spirit); blue flowers, such as violets, hyacinths, hydrangeas, lavender, or anything else available in season; 1 golden and 1 blue taper.

MOON PHASE: *Anytime from new to full.*

Perform this spell when you are feeling happy and positive. Make a circle in the middle of your busiest room by placing the blue and gold cords in semicircles opposite each other, so that they join, thereby making a complete circle of two different colors. Write your name on the paper, place it in the middle, and put near it an emblem of the work you do—make it a pen if you write a lot, a book if you study or teach, a domestic item if you tend the house, something edible if you cook, paint or fabric if you're creative, or anything else that readily springs to mind that is symbolic of your professional life. Now, make an arrangement of all the flowers, and put them in the center of the circle as well. Last of all, light the candles and place them in the circle.

Walk once around the circle, asking for security and pleasure in your working life; ask that you contribute utility, that your contribution be positive, and that you be valued fairly for it. Look out at the sky, and think of the busy universe; of the world stirring around you; of all the balanced activity, refined by thousands of years of interconnection. See yourself in the midst of this web.

Lift the flowers out of the circle, kiss them, and place them on a central table; the next day, transfer them to the place where you work. Take your cords and make a big bow from them, tying them anywhere that makes you smile (a wastebasket is fun!). The candles need only burn for about an hour—thereafter, light them from time to time to ask for blessings on your work.

Remember to grow blue flowers in a pot at work, and if you like, tie the cords together around the big pot. YOUR WORK LIFE WILL BLOSSOM.

ENCHANTMENT

WILLOW MOON

THE

WILLOW MOON, KNOWN AS THE WITCHES'

MOON, RULES THE RICH SPRING PERIOD FROM MID-

APRIL TO EARLY MAY. NOW, WE EXPLORE THE CRUCIAL ASPECT OF

SELF-EMPOWERMENT, WHICH HAS SIGNIFICANT IMPACT ON EVERY AREA OF

LIFE. SYMBOLS FOR PERSONAL STRENGTH AND TALISMANS FOR PERSONAL

FULFILLMENT ARE USED. THE MASTER SPELL IS ONE TO "ENCHANT"—TO WIN ANYONE

OVER COMPLETELY TO YOUR POINT OF VIEW! THIS INCLUDES LOVE, BUSINESS, AND

SOCIAL FUNCTIONS, BUT BEING "ENCHANTED" ALSO CONCERNS THE PASSIONS, AND YOU

WILL LEARN HOW TO ADD PASSION TO YOUR LIFE AND HOW TO KEEP UP A MAGICAL DANCE,

ENCHANTING THE SENSES WITH SENSUALITY. THIS IS THE MOMENT TO DISCOVER YOUR

PERSONAL CHARISMA—AND, AS SUCH, IS THE MOST IMPORTANT PHASE FOR THE SELF.

THE FEAST DAY THAT FALLS IN THIS PERIOD IS MAY DAY, OR BELTANE. THE "LUSTY

MONTH OF MAY" WAS ALWAYS CONNECTED WITH FERTILITY RITES AND THE

PASSAGE FROM VIRGINAL SPRING TO VOLUPTUOUS LATE SPRING'S FULL-

BODIED WARMTH. MAGICAL RITUAL NOW IS FOR THE PHYSICAL

SIDE OF LOVE—SO TAKE YOUR LOVED ONE TO THE

FLOWER-FILLED WOODS, AND ENJOY!

MAY DAY: THE FEAST OF BELTANE. This is the most important Wicca feast of the year, next to Samhain (Hallowe'en). The latter was the New Year (and ushering-in of the winter). This is the start of the summer year, and the celebration of the most fertile, prosperous, optimistic moment in the calendar.

The name seems to derive from the Scottish sun deity, Bel, or the Celtic god of fire, and reflects the importance of the warmer months (then and now). It is also thought that the word derives from that for a "balefire"—the bonfire that was always lit on May Day eve (April 30th). Veneration of the may tree and the maypole both spring from the powerful magic of tree worship. The maiden turns here from innocence to experience; this is the festival of sexuality. Once, for blessings and fertility, a may tree, or hawthorn shrub, was planted in front of nearly every dwelling in the country. Those who couldn't plant a tree gathered green vegetation, beautiful boughs of flowers and greenery, and fastened them to the doors of their homes, bringing the providential blessing of the tree spirit. Traditionally, for powerful magical luck, the branches should be gathered after midnight on May Day Eve. Unbridled passion was completely endorsed at this time, and couples would spend the night outdoors in the woods, testing their fertility.

On May Day itself (May 1st), one person of each sex was anointed with the special powers of bringing "green" magic into the fields and the houses: they were the May Queen and the Green Man, also called the Whitsuntide King, Green George, or Jack-in-the-Green. His day was April 23rd, and he was transformed in Christianity into St. George (of dragon fame), whose day is marked on April 23rd.

If you want to celebrate Beltane, bring May Day rituals alive again to evoke the powerful magic of the past. For witches and Wiccans, these rituals include: the wearing of green; the purchase of a new tree and endowment with magic and spells as you plant it; the decking of boughs of green in the home, office, and gardens, with ritual incantation for both personal fertility and communal fertility (prosperity); and/or the placing of a may wreath opposite the door or gate to avert bad weather. And most magically, the utilization of the mystical "crack between the worlds" ushered in at Beltane—here, and at Samhain, there is the possibility of a glimpse into the fairy world.

At this point winter is defeated by its rival summer, just as love rivals may go into battle for one prized heart wearing a token of birch leaves. The May Queen is an incarnation on earth of the full-blown spring goddess, and her Italian cousin is Flora, bringer of spring flowers and symbol of full summer fertility and love. Even the Phrygian sibyl was an ancestress of the spring goddess—her particular festival being "hilaria," which was a romp of sensuality!

May will always be associated with love of the flirtatious, extra-marital kind. This is not the divine marriage, but the moment of the senses overflowing with ripeness. Thus, to go "a-maying" was a euphemism for gathering may flowers from the hawthorn and tasting the pleasures of illicit love—a licentiousness almost condoned by custom!

So why not take a picnic to the woods with the one you love and "observe some May revels." Pack some body balms and massage oils to enjoy practicing sensuality and flirting under your very own "greenwood tree." Lovemaking out of doors has always been condoned at this time, so be inventive!

WILLOW MOON—MOON OF ENCHANTMENT. Colors: PURPLE, WISTERIA, LAVENDER. Scents: LAVENDER, SANDALWOOD, BENZOIN. Number: 5. The language of love and the passions draws heavily on magic. We are "charmed" by someone initially, "enchanted" perhaps; and the first flush of deeper love certainly feels like a spell that is working in spite of logic or the banal demands of our normal lives.

"A little still she strove, and much repented,
And whispering 'I will ne'er consent'—consented."
FROM CANTO I, "DON JUAN"
LORD BYRON

The feeling of falling in love lifts us above the humdrum; everything gray takes on a sunnier face. This is possibly because our senses are, in a way, "intoxicated"; and if we can recapture that for ourselves, and promote it in others, our lives can be transposed from pastels to bright colors at will.

ENCHANTMENT HAS A PLACE IN EVERY ASPECT OF OUR LIVES. We can grow an "enchanted" garden, luring creatures and eliciting beauty from it on a paradisical scale (even in a few square yards). We can enchant in our working lives, to keep others happy and cooperative, and business ticking over quietly. We can enchant family and friends with simple measures that will add depth and color to their lives. We can enchant our lovers to add dimension, beauty, and durability to the relationship.

What we cannot do is enchant anyone for the purpose of gaining power "over" them—by which I mean holding them "in thrall." Magic must always be an invitation to greater richness, a bolder tapestry of life: it cannot be a license to manipulate others for your gain. This would, quite simply, be an abuse of trust. Never convince yourself that it is fair to diminish someone else's life in order to enhance your own: getting someone fired in order to take their job, or spreading gossip to undermine another's confidence for your own gain, is not the work of a white witch—and is a recipe for disaster.

That said, we will examine the ways in which we can use enchantment to improve our lot. And for this, we need the willow tree and the willow moon. It is the tree sacred to witches, and some will even say that they would rather not have it in the house, because of its immense power and, of course, its association with "weeping." But it is this very association with human feeling that gives it that special something in white magic.

THE NATURE OF WILLOW

Willow grows along riverbanks, ditches, waterways, fens, and other marshy land where water is abundant. Water is the element that governs the emotions, so this places willow symbolically in the realm of "feeling," as it understands and incorporates that medium of emotion into its system. Because of its sensitivity to water, it is one of the chief trees used in water divination, and this alone was enough to place it high in the esteem of the Druids and Celts. In fact, the willow has been revered for centuries by many cultures for its bark, which contains salicylic acid—the basis of aspirin. Drinking willow bark tea was a cure for fevers; the leaves as well as the bark have long been used to treat pain, headache, inflammations, even rheumatism and arthritis. For its aspirin-like uses, the tree was always one of the favorite medicinal herbs used by the healers of ancient people—witches being no exception.

Making a knot of willow harnesses its strength and proclaims the spell-maker a witch of the blood. Willow is there for your use, and for me symbolizes a maiden with tresses reaching all the way to the earth, incorporating the waters of time—and thus wisdom—in its sap. Learn to respect the willow's power: but do not fear it. Think of this as an electric current, and handle it wisely.

A true witch, then, will want a willow tree growing in their garden, or in a pot on their roof or balcony. Get advice from a garden centre or good nursery, choose a large enough pot, water the plant well, and it will love you like a human friend.

THE WILLOW KNOT

This is a step toward enchantment. Bend a small, soft, pliable piece of just-green willow gently into a knot like a figure eight, and as you do this make a little prayer to honor the goddess (which can simply mean that you will consider the patterns and needs of Mother Earth). Think of yourself as part of the chain of other wise exponents of the craft going before you, and as you weave your knot with your prayer, think loving thoughts to all those who cross your mind—including difficult landladies and sharp-tongued in-laws! In other words, weave a spell of magical enchantment as you tie your little knot. Think musical, happy thoughts: see yourself, like Orpheus in the Greek legend, taming savage entities with the enchanting sound. This knot will find its way into our master spell and variations, but you can also use it in "everyday" magic by placing it among the daily tools of your profession, in your pocket as you meet people, in your home for protection, or even under the tablecloth if you have an important dinner engagement. It gives you bewitching power, good humor, wisdom, and grace—and *these are the elements of self-empowerment on a major scale.*

THE SCENTS OF ENCHANTMENT. Scent can bewitch at a stroke. Our brains are especially responsive to scents that arouse our passions because, at the most basic level, it is this that ensures the continued reproduction of the species. Some scents make us feel sexually aroused instantly, others entice our interest, and still others make us feel good in the company of the people with whom we share the scent. We must therefore learn to use the right one at the right time!

TUBEROSE is the most wonderful scent. It is difficult to come by, and you may have to settle for a tuberose-based perfume, or at best a perfume oil (this is not pure oil, but carries the perfume of the flower). I buy tuberose in Paris; it is forbiddingly expensive, but a little goes a very long way. I save it for very special occasions when nothing else will quite do. A tiny drop will counteract irritability and emotional conflict; it also arouses sensuality, motivates, invites spontaneity, and can even transform an introverted person into a more outgoing personality. When you consider that all these effects will be felt by both the wearer of the oil or perfume and those who smell it, you can see its true potential. My advice would definitely be that it is worth a trip to Paris!

JASMINE is related to tuberose, and some of the effects are similar. It has the power to make you feel almost hypnotized: sexual, confident, inspired, near-euphoric. It also counters some of the negative traits that hinder passion, such as anxiety, poor self-esteem, jealousy, guilt, and tension. It can even dispose of feelings of frigidity, which explains its popularity as an aphrodisiac scent in the East. Again, my advice is that it is well worth its high price tag.

GARDENIA oil has almost all the properties of the above. To ensure a supply, grow pots of gardenias. If you have a romantic dinner planned and want a straight ticket to the boudoir without even getting to the dessert, place a flowering plant squarely in the middle of the table. You're halfway there. Put another cut flower just by your bed. Voilà! If you are lucky enough to find the perfume oil, or even the essential oil, you will discover it to be a wonderful scent to help anyone overcome feelings of fear and depression about past failures in bed or in relationships. It is also a good oil for those who have previously suffered violence in a sexual or an emotional climate.

YLANG-YLANG has a gigantic reputation as an aphrodisiac and is the oil most closely synonymous with sensual warmth and joyfulness. It generates a feeling of self-confidence, awakens those who are excessively fatigued, and also combats chronic shyness. What more could you possibly ask for?

LAVENDER adds compassion and gentleness to the mix. Instead of inflaming the passions, it excites more gently, though it does rejuvenate and comfort after a difficult day. Lavender is marvelous to use in tandem with other oils if there is an element of forgiveness, or tentativeness, to counteract. It is also wonderful just to strew the fresh herb (grow it for this purpose alone) around your bed. It looks great on crisp white linen, and after lifting you to dizzy, sensual heights, it will relax you for a perfect sleep in the afterglow of passion. Perhaps this is the secret of happy life in southern France?

SO, HOW SHOULD YOU INCORPORATE THESE
SCENTS INTO YOUR SORCERY OF PASSION?
Set the mood for intimate dinners by dispersing the scent via a
burner; bathe in your own personal mixture of these scents (or
keep one pure); scent the sheets; spray some on a lightbulb; infuse
the candles with a little fragrance; dab some on your pulse
points, properly diluted, or dilute the scents in water (4 drops
essential oil to 10 fl. oz. water) in an atomizer; last but not least,
spray a little on your hair or into your car or briefcase. This is
pheromone manipulation of the most serious kind.

The scents to make another passionate, and that are thus
the right choice for sensuality shared with another, are expensive:
but there really is no substitute for quality.

THE COLORS OF ENCHANTMENT
LAVENDER appears in the color chart as well as on the olfactory
shortlist: the purples are the colors of power and passion. It is
difficult to refuse a person who is in control of purple, and this
is a point to remember. If you cannot feel strong in purple, and
sense instead that it is wearing you, tone it down to lavender
or wisteria.

Tips for a successful social function, speech, or party
would be to spread the color purple profusely around the room,
disperse the scents listed opposite, and tie a great knot of
willow over the threshold like mistletoe. I like purple balloons
into which a few drops of scent have been placed. When they burst
(and they always do after a while), a shower of joy breaks into the
room and rains sunshine on the proceedings.

Flowers chosen in these hues are as apt for the boardroom
as the bedroom; ribbons should find a place, too. If you tie
silverware for an executive lunch with purple ribbon, everyone
will wait to hear from you. You will also gain a reputation for an
interesting design style!

THE SYMBOLS OF ENCHANTMENT

- The strongest visual encouragement for someone to listen to you, and attend to all you say and do, is the WILLOW KNOT. Wear it around your neck or pinned to a coat. You will receive some interesting inquiries about it before the day is over!

- The other main symbols for enchanting are a SPIDER'S WEB (which you might get made into jewelry), and large MOONSTONES—which resemble the color, size, and density of the willow moon. Charge their power first from the moon's rays, and wear them with a special prayer in mind. Wish on them with great belief and positivity. Never doubt.

- The ACORN and OAK LEAF are other symbols of confidence and have the power to enchant. Carry one with a sense that you have a secret weapon against all negativity.

- Lastly, a KEY, tied with a small scrap of purple ribbon, is a powerful talisman indeed with which to enchant a person and wish that they will hear every word you say, hanging on each one. Place the key on a beautiful silver key ring, charged with the moon's light. This will make a very personal but powerful attractor of magical thought and translator of your own vibration.

ENCHANTMENT IN EVERYDAY LIFE

If you wish to work a little enchantment daily, to gently turn up the volume of passion in your relationship, or simply to make others in your home feel loved, go a little crazy with purple or lavender ribbons and fragrance in odd places.

Tie back your bed curtains with purple ribbons; tie purple ribbons around the silverware you place at dinner; trail a purple ribbon (and candles alongside) from your living room to your bed; and tie a purple (or possibly red) ribbon around some intimate part of your body. Hang lavender-stuffed slippers above your bed, then wear the shoes the next day for bewitching power: people will fall at your feet!

If you simply want to keep your dwelling purified and tease visitors about the emblematic significance of it, you could cut a "wand" (no more than 15–20 inches long) from a birch tree on a full moon, tie a beautiful bow of flame-red around it, and place it above a mantelpiece, on a bookshelf, or anywhere else in your home that pleases you.

MASTER SPELL: TO ENCHANT AND GAIN SELF-EMPOWERMENT. This spell is requisite to any really important task you have to fulfill concerning your own life. It is relevant (possibly in tandem with a particular love spell) to sallying forth to meet a long-lost lover, or following an argument; it is beneficent when you are applying for a job or taking an exam; it is imperative if you have to win someone over to your way of thinking. DO NOT ABUSE IT....

YOU WILL NEED
A sprig of willow, tied into a simple knot; 5 candles in a purple (tending to wisteria) hue; any of the oils described in this chapter, plus peony, wisteria, or carnation perfume oil; 1/2 yard of purple ribbon; purple underwear—bought specially for this occasion!

MOON PHASE: *Waxing*

The night before your important appointment, tie the willow sprig gently into a simple knot, and place it by your bedside. Place your right hand through the knot (or, if you have only a small piece, place your index finger into it) and "breathe in" the colors and scent of the willow. From your toes upward, imagine the little pliable twig bringing you energy, hope, and confidence.

Next morning, before your appointment, light the candles and place them next to the willow, then sprinkle a few drops of the oil on the willow knot itself. Tie the ribbon loosely around one of the candles, and make a very calm direction:

"All that follows from this day, Will rest within my power, Though magic, such, is pure child's play, My good grace shall not sour."

Now envision, very simply, a brief picture of the resolution you desire: someone shaking your hand to conclude the business, or a love holding you with warmth and renewed passion, or an exam passing off without difficulty, and so on. Stand up and bow slightly to the burning candles, then dress—beginning with the special undergarments, which you should first sprinkle with the passion oils described on page 82.

As you put on your clothes, look at the candles and see the success you want attending you; imagine everything will go your way, and promise not to abuse this. Finally, blow out the candles, untie the ribbon, and tie it instead around your stockinged thigh (or wrist, if you prefer), then put a dab of the oil on your pulse points. Pop the willow knot—the most important talisman—into a pocket or your purse, and quietly repeat the words above as you do so. The outcome of your event should now be everything you could wish for. NO ONE CAN REFUSE YOU TODAY!

DISENCHANTMENT

HAWTHORN MOON

THERE

COMES A MOMENT WHEN YOU MUST TURN

OFF UNDESIRABLE FEELINGS. THIS NEED IS MAGICALLY

SYMBOLIZED BY THIS MOON, THE MOON OF HINDRANCE, WHICH

COVERS THE PERIOD MID-MAY TO EARLY JUNE. THIS CHAPTER CONCERNS

SPELLS TO DISENCHANT, WHICH ARE A VITAL PART OF MAGIC. IF SOMEONE IS

BEING IMPOSSIBLY PERSISTENT ABOUT SOMETHING YOU REALLY DON'T WISH TO DO,

LOOK HERE FOR HELP. THIS ADVICE IS FOR THOSE WHO BELIEVE (OR KNOW) THAT THEY

ARE ATTRACTING ATTENTION FROM AN UNDESIRABLE QUARTER—A PAST LOVER, A FRIEND'S

PARTNER, A BOSS, OR SOMEONE ELSE TRYING TO ABUSE A POSITION OF AUTHORITY. IT MAY

EQUALLY BE THAT YOU ARE FEELING AN ATTRACTION YOURSELF TO SOMEONE ILL-ADVISED,

AND IT WOULD BE WELL TO LOOK TO MAGICAL WAYS OF NIPPING UNWISE ATTRACTIONS

IN THE BUD. THE MOON OF HINDRANCE ALSO TAKES CARE OF UNWELCOME

INTRUDERS: PERFORM THESE MAGICAL RITES TO MINIMIZE THE THREAT OF UN-

WANTED GUESTS IN YOUR HOME (EVEN ANIMALS!) OR TO PUT UP A MAGICAL

BARRIER BETWEEN YOUR SERENITY AND THE OUTSIDE WORLD. THE

MASTER SPELL IS DESIGNED TO RID YOU OF A PAST LOVE

AFFAIR OR DISENCHANT AN UNWANTED

ADMIRER.

HAWTHORN MOON—MOON OF DISENCHANTMENT. Colors: ROSE-PINK, WHITISH-PINK. Scents: CAMPHOR, MINT, PINE, PEPPER. Number: 6.

There is a double nuance to the beautiful hawthorn tree. One face it wears is that of the smiling, beguiling may flower that we discovered in the chapter on ENCHANTMENT; as such, it understands well the subjects of love, flirtation, and unruly passion. Its other face, however, is of the greater concern to us here; for hawthorn is the first choice, in England, for creating an impenetrable barrier between farm fields, or constructing a castle wall of protection around the family home. If you wish to keep anything out, choose thorn!

"And on a day we meet to walk the line,
   And set the wall between us once again."
"MENDING WALL"
ROBERT FROST

In a sense, it is this compassionate ambivalence that makes hawthorn the right choice for working magic that requires an emotional understanding of feeling and attraction, while realizing that, for whatever reason, it should be curtailed. This moon and this tree wish no harm on the other party—as with all white magic. If you are going to ask that someone to respect your boundaries, you must do so with charm, grace, and sensitivity. Hence, the flowering thorn: it is relevant and indeed significant that the tree flowers throughout the whole period of the hawthorn moon. Thus, tread softly on another's dreams! Soften your thorny words of protection with flowers of friendship, and lovingly ask that the other party desist! Most of the time you will prefer to enchant people—THE HAWTHORN IS FOR USE ONLY WHEN THIS HAS GOTTEN OUT OF HAND!

THE HAWTHORN KNOT

As with the enchanter's knot made of willow (see page 81), this is a talisman you will need to keep with you if you are waging a little war of attrition with a persistent suitor; it can also be used in any situation where you are trying to disenchant someone. Pick a little piece of hawthorn branch (take care of your fingers!) on a waxing moon; you will use it on a waning moon in spell making.

Work at night, and ask that your thorn knot protect you from unwelcome attentions, unsolicited advances, or unwise thoughts on your own part toward anyone else. Using gloves, if necessary, weave your thorn into a beautiful figure-eight knot. The "eight" protects from an infinite number of possibilities; but if you cannot work an eight knot, make a simple loop (like a ring) which will keep for eternity. As you knot, say, *"I wish no other being harm, but wish myself safe and secure in the loop of my own identity."* Place the knot somewhere safe, such as inside a lidded box. You want to be able to take the knot out at will and choose when to use it, rather than have it work as a constant repellant.

THE SCENTS OF RESTRAINT. If you need to restrain the thoughts and actions of another, or if you need to exercise self-restraint, the scent must be one of abruptness, a discouraging fragrance—one that will brace you or your adversary and wake you up to the messages that are being given.

MINT is the place to start: in fact, research indicates that mint works as a deterrent to animals in the garden, helps to mollify wild dogs, and signals the brain to think intelligently rather than emotionally. Many mixtures based on mint are worthy of a place in the weaponry of refusing love.

BLACK PEPPER also wakes a suitor out of reverie and asks that they attend to the words actually being spoken—not those they would like to imagine were forthcoming. Thus, for instance, if you were to have dinner with someone you really wanted to deter from making advances, a mixture of black pepper and mint spritzed onto your wrist and pulse points would be quite a turn-off.

PINE has a strongly disinfectant smell, and is bracing rather than sensual. This is a good choice if you are experiencing harassment at work: you will be equated with the cleaner, and will not appear nearly so desirable!

CAMPHOR is famous for its capacity to deter anything living. It is sometimes hard to find camphor oil itself, but you can use camphor-based ointments, or burn the leaves from a camphor laurel tree to release the scent, or at worst use mothballs, which are based on camphor. Camphorated oil may be available from your pharmacy, as it is used as a decongestant.

Use any of these oils as inhalants from which to meditate dissuasive thoughts to the party causing you problems.

Sit in the center of a ring of pinkish-white light, cast by six pink candles and six white, placed alternately, and envision your subject. Place a heavy beam of light between you—dividing rather than connecting you. Scent that beam with the fragrances around you: imagine a great peppermint stick of pink and white light creating a "wall" between you. Or draw a line of pepper in white light; or surround the other person in a glow of warm light to wish them well, but scent that light with clouds of camphor.

If you understand that the colors you use are made up of loving shades, you will realize how important compassion is. It is almost like saying, *"If you love me, let me go."* Asking someone to release you in a hostile manner is, psychologically, more like an invitation to their ego to prove that they can overcome your lack of feeling. Asking that someone respect your wishes, while remaining gracious, is harder to deny. Of course, along with that politeness there is the scent of refusal. YOU MUST ENVISION THE EFFECT VERY POWERFULLY, FOR ONLY THEN WILL YOUR BARRIER BE RESPECTED.

HONORING THE MAY THORN

There is a strange duality about the hawthorn, or may tree. Because the honoring of the god and goddess in Pagan mythology occurred in May, when the tree was at full stretch, blossoming its heart out, the hawthorn came to be seen as synonymous with blessings from the gods. Then, too, the month of May was connected with revels and witchcraft, and the tree was said to be enchanted, so that cutting boughs of hawthorn was a possible way of letting fairy folk into the house.

The may tree was a visual symbol of beauty and enchantment; its thorn was a symbol of obstruction. At the end of the May festival, the god and goddess were "killed off" as part of the ritual of progress that would develop over the continuing summer—eventually to lead to a renewed life cycle the following year. For this reason, the hawthorn was associated with hope and fertility, but was also an omen of death; the tree is both lucky and unlucky. It is this paradox that encompasses the hawthorn tree/moon as one of love and of hindrance. Always remember this dichotomy when you are working magic to repel someone. There must be love and positivity combined with your dissuasive intention.

To protect yourself from misplaced affection, include thorn leaves in your salads, or put them in your sandwiches for work. The tree was actually known as "bread-and-cheese" because the leaves taste so good used in this way—and you will know the consumption of the plant also has a witchy significance! If a co-worker is becoming distastefully frisky or officiously attentive with you, make them a sandwich of the same ingredients, uttering a few words to the effect of "Back!" as you make it. If they eat the leaves, they will begin to take on the idea that their flirtations are unwelcome.

THINKING UP A BARRIER

The most important place to begin your siege warfare—and keep another out of your garden—is in your head. As with all magic, a practical assessment of the situation should be followed by a symbolic refusal of continuance magically (and, as relevant, a physical barrier being placed between you and the other party). Your mind can do much of this work by carefully aimed thought. Here your visualization skills are in demand. You must harness what you have already learned and concentrate your thoughts on gently but firmly refusing the advances that you don't want. Employ the colors and scents of refusal, and send a powerful, polite request to the other party to cease their actions.

DISCOURAGING YOUR OWN FEELINGS. From time to time, temptations arise to provoke the most constant of lovers. It may be that you are part of a normally happy pair, but that someone else has simply stolen your attention momentarily. Or possibly your own partner is too busy to pay you proper due. Or, you are tired, lonely, or in need of an ego boost.

In such situations, sit down and discuss with yourself (a) what is the cause of your new interest in someone else, and (b) whether or not this will ultimately cost you all that you love. Sometimes, just pausing and assessing what you will lose, or what pain you may be entering into, is enough to dissuade you (at least mentally) from active pursuit of the tempting new personality.

This may be one of the most important things you will ever do to save yourself immense pain, hurt, and mischief. Scent your room with mint and one other fragrance chosen from those described on page 91, light one pink and one white candle, and tie several white ribbons around the room. Find a piece of hawthorn, or rose thorn if you have no access to a thorn tree, and place it between the two candles.

Now imagine the other person's face and pretend you can see it through the ring of your thorn knot. Send it love, but send it also a warning not to get any closer. Give yourself the same mental warning. Breathe in the scent of restraint, tie a white ribbon around your wrist or finger, and padlock your consciousness to the other person by literally envisioning a padlock on your heart.

Then dispel your own amorous feelings by quietly drawing the other person to mind, fixing on one (perhaps the only) part of their physical appearance or personality that you don't like, and exaggerating its importance in your mind. If you don't much like their nose, for example, magnify it into a caricature of itself—so that it makes you laugh. Or, if you don't like the way they dress, exaggerate this style.

Finally, send the person a feeling of good friendship, so that you avoid the idea that they are "forbidden fruit." Make sure that you congratulate yourself on your very strong will—and do not be afraid to recognize that it is an act of will to terminate your feelings.

If you can spend sufficient time on this now, and truly talk yourself out of any attraction, you may save a great deal of worry and ensure instead a future of genuine, warm friendship.

OTHER TIPS

- If you are concerned that someone in your office is getting ideas about you, mix a little camphor oil blended with one or two of the other oils described on page 91 and spray this around your desk. Tie a white ribbon around your chair to keep yourself "free" from others. Place a pink candle, scented with your chosen anti-attractant, near your front door, and then light it, asking (anyone in particular, or everyone in general) respecfully to keep their distance from you.

- Spray your car with the above mixture to keep thieves away. Do the same to your flowerpots and garden beds to communicate your lack of hospitality to cats and dogs.

- Wearing pink and/or white clothes is a good shield against attention; if you have an appointment with someone you don't wish to encourage, wear these colors and place a thorn knot in your pocket. Donning some scent made up from three of those described on page 91 will seal the fatal unattraction!

- If you feel that you are "under siege" from someone who is taking liberties with you in their thoughts, place a beautiful sprig of blossoming hawthorn, or a knot woven from the tree, above your front door, tied into a rose-pink or pinky-white silk kerchief. This is also a good safeguard against theft. If you tie a willow twig in with it, intruders will come to no good end if they cross your threshold!

MASTER SPELL: **TO DISENCHANT A PAST LOVER OR UNWANTED ADMIRER.**

If you want to ease away someone who has impossible hopes for either a renewed relationship with you or a cherished but completely unreturned interest in your affection, perform this spell with feeling, but firm denial.

YOU WILL NEED

3 rose-pink and 3 white candles; a few drops of pine and camphor oils (substitute another second choice if you cannot find camphor); a piece of hawthorn cut from a living tree; a very small blank notebook, with your "harasser's" name written on the first page; a photograph of the person, if you have one, or an item belonging to them if not; a sprig of peppermint (fresh grown, or bought packaged from the supermarket); a small birdcage, or other pet cage (even a nesting box would do, as long as it has a door you can leave open); 1 yard each of pink and white ribbon.

MOON PHASE: *Work on a full moon, and finish the spell within 24 hours so that the moon is waning by the end of the period.*

Form a large triangle shape with the candles, to symbolize that there are effectively three people in this spell: you, the unwanted lover, and another person to whom you would like your admirer to transfer their affection. Anoint the candles with a drop of each oil a few minutes before you light them, and say the name of your "harasser" as you do this. Take the thorn, tied in a large ring-shaped knot, and pass it over each candle in turn, saying firmly, *"[name], take your affections and burn for another; Though I will be friends I cannot be your lover. I wish you well with somebody new, But there can be nothing between me and you."* IMAGINE KISSING THE PERSON VERY CHASTELY, AND SEE YOURSELF WALKING AWAY.

While the candles burn, write the person's name in the notebook, sprinkle oils onto the page, and tape in the photograph or item belonging to them. Draw a wing upon the page, to symbolize flight from each other, and imagine the person running swiftly away from you to another life. Pass the peppermint and the thorn knot through the light of the candles, repeat the words, then place the peppermint in the notebook near the name and photo. Look at the picture and slip the "ring" of thorn onto your marriage finger; explain in your own words that this union, so desired by the other, is not wished for by you. Slip off the thorn ring and place it on the page, open.

Finally, put the notebook into the little cage, and leave the door open. Visualize one last, powerful image of the person who likes you departing from the cage they have made for themselves in wanting your love, and ask that they fly out. Sprinkle the cage with a little of the oil.

The next day, take the notebook and tie it with the ribbons, enclosing all that has gone inside (photo, name, oils, peppermint sprig—but not the hawthorn). Place the "ring" on your finger one last time, and take the book to moving water. Imagine you are freeing a caged bird as you drop the book in the water and watch it rush away. Take the "ring" off your finger and say the words opposite one last time. See the bond depart; see the other party freed, and you as well. WISH THEM WELL ELSEWHERE.

SECURITY

OAK MOON

This chapter centers on oak, the moon of strength and security. We will examine magic for protection and security, especially financial security, and work a master spell for fertility. We adopt talismans for everyday power and personal strength, many of which take their inspiration from the mighty oak tree. Ancient rituals connected with midsummer, the solstice (on June 21, within the period—early June to early July—ruled by this moon), and the certainty of a good crop came under the aegis of this moon. The earth was pregnant, but the safe delivery of a healthy and bountiful harvest had to be worked for. Thus in life, we must not rest on our laurels, but put in the effort to assure continuing strength and surety. This is the time of year dedicated to cultivating and applying our knowledge for utmost security. The month of June was named "Oak" ("Duir") in the Celtic calendar, and Juno was the consort of Jupiter, who was associated with the oak—the king of trees. Thus her emblem is the June, or mid summer, moon—his is the oak sun.

OAK MOON—MOON OF STRENGTH AND SECURITY. Colors: BRICK, EARTH, WHITE. Scents: GERANIUM, BAY, FRANKINCENSE, SANDALWOOD. Number: 7. The oak is tried and true; its wood is dense and close-grown, and it endures for several hundred years growing in the forest; similarly, its wood is the strongest and most enduring for building. Thus the tree is a symbol of strength, wisdom, endurance, and security. Oak wood is the most powerful fuel of fire and is seen in conjunction with the most powerful sun—THE "SECURE" SUN!

"She kneels beneath the huge oak tree
 And in silence prayeth she."
"CHRISTABEL"
SAMUEL TAYLOR COLERIDGE

The subject of personal security embraces many things: it could include self-confidence, financial stability, happiness in love, a safe place in which to live; but in the specific realm of the witches' working calendar, this security is most strongly related to the protection of home and family and financial security. Tied in with this is the concept at the heart of the number "7" (for this is the seventh moon), which is concerned with the intellect and analysis—qualities that are directly involved with the maintenance of financial security.

For centuries in Pagan magic and worship, oak bark, acorns, and leaves have been used medicinally, as well as in fertility rites, divination magic, and prosperity and protection magic.

The oak could almost be equated with anything positive: for this reason, the acorn is often used as a central motif in all types of spell, and for the magical path that represents magic in our everyday lives. Oak was the most sacred tree of all to the Druids, and in many English churches the vaulting is made from curved oak timbers; indeed, the columns of the nave seem almost to resemble overhanging branches in a great forest. This perhaps recalls the time when the forest was actually the religious grove of Druid worship: nature herself was the venerated force.

This, then, is the time to employ nature to the full and venerate our own life force—our strength, security, and positivity. By doing this effectively, we can turn our lives along a route of good fortune and sunshine. If thought is the most powerful element we have with which to direct our future, we must think up powerfully positive thoughts to determine the extent of our happiness, inner calm, and power to attain.

As with all magic, the effectiveness of your magic making will depend on your capacity to think powerful thoughts and to visualize well. By now you will have become more used to doing this as part of spell making; you should find the exercise of sending protective light in conjunction with spells for security very easy to achieve. *If we think positively, we can design for ourselves the lives we want. . . .*

BEGINNING WITH THOUGHT

To be adept, our thoughts must be well directed, focused, and unflinching. Begin by releasing any negativity from the past. Do not castigate yourself for previous failures or weaknesses, but go past them. Remind yourself that burning a cake once does not mean you will always do so: you have learned more about what will make the cake burn, so you can improve the next try.

SO IN MAGIC: let go completely of past misfortunes, cease to think of yourself in any negative way at all, and set your course for a more fulfilled and prosperous future. Certain scents will help you do this; so will color. Strangely enough, beating past failures is often simply a case of assessing an impasse quickly and letting go of the dead wood, rather than hanging on to "no-win" situations. It may also be largely a matter of making the decision to go out and meet life, rather than expecting everything to come to you on a platter. If you take a shining, positive face out into the world, you will soon discover that you meet with a more positive response from all around you.

Move toward greater strength in your life, armed with talismans for positivity, by being decisive in small projects and taking gentle, unhurried steps toward attaining each one. You will make no progress if you set yourself no goals. The adage that you get more out of life if you put more in is, simply, all too true!

SCENTS FOR OPTIMISM

Many scents are associated with making us feel more positive; the woody aromas, such as pine, cedar, rosewood, and cypress, are all scents that help us to feel clearheaded, secure, and well grounded. But if you want to surround yourself with scents that have a traditional role in positive thought, those valued in the East—frankincense and sandalwood—can make you feel quite inspirational. It is worth using a diffuser, or scented candles, in conjunction with sending your light and thinking positively.

So, a simple routine for preparing the ground for a successful, secure situation would be as follows. Consider the end product you would like to reach: if you are timid about a meeting, an interview, a date, an exam, a social occasion, a speech you have to give, or whatever, think clearly about arriving—or receiving a guest—with a sense of total self-confidence, poise, and inner security. Now diffuse one of the above oils into the atmosphere from a burner, or bathe in a combination of several, and inhale deeply, calmly, confidently, and rhythmically while focusing on the desired outcome. By doing this, you are preparing the way—rehearsing, if you like—for the real thing.

Geranium and bay are also wonderful scents for strength, optimism, and security. If you are performing in a play, taking a driving test—anything, in fact, where you need to feel sure of yourself—dilute these (a few drops of each in a base oil, such as sweet almond) and wear them on your wrist or as a perfume. *You will be shining, confident, and focused from beginning to end!*

THE COLORS OF POSITIVITY AND STRENGTH

Well might you expect to see the colors of positivity and security coming from the brilliant primaries, or bold, bright colors. In fact, interestingly, the colors associated with strength are the colors of the earth—the browns, especially brick. Is it because they connote solidity, dependability, rather than passing dazzle? I don't know the answer, but earth colors definitely make us feel secure. Wearing browns can make us feel more grounded and reliable. Use a shade of brown that speaks to you; "brick" could go all the way to a Chinese brick red!

When you are sallying forth into the world and want to feel secure and optimistic, apart from wearing browns you could tie ribbons in the brownish hues all about you: on your wrist, in your car, on your briefcase or purse. Don't worry if it seems eccentric: this translates to others as difference and creativity!

SECURITY MAGIC IN EVERYDAY LIFE. You can incorporate the symbology of the oak moon into your daily life to encourage a positive outcome on a regular basis. NEVER LEAVE HOME WITHOUT AN ACORN!

This powerful talisman is sure to attract growing strength in your life. If you can't get hold of a real one, ask a jeweler to make you one in silver or gold. Put it in your pocket, tie it to your key ring, attach it to your purse or billfold, or place it in a prominent place at the office or in your home. Charge it first with real strength from a full summery moon—oak if possible—and imagine beautiful light filling the little acorn, infusing it with power and strength. Think of this little "battery," full of energy, now being in your control.

CHOOSE ANY WAY OF PLACING THIS POWERFUL TALISMAN IN YOUR LIFE THAT FITS IN WITH YOUR LIFESTYLE.

• Soak in a bath of oak leaves, and draw in (almost hypnotically) a feeling of control and inner power. If you can get some oak bark, you will find bathing in it very therapeutic: *the bark has a long history of use as a medicine with antiseptic and astringent properties.*

• It may be possible to find acorn-shaped finials for drapery or shade pulls, because the oak tree has long been associated with protection of the house, particularly from thunder and lightning, because it was dedicated to the Scandinavian god Thor.

• Design your own jewelry around acorns, oak leaves, or oak wood, and pin it as a brooch for an added boost.

• Decorate your house with oak motifs, for continuing strength and positivity. Gather oak leaves at an appropriate time, spray them gold if you wish, and put them on plates; make place mats with them, or press them in a picture frame.

• Find an old piece of oak wood and incorporate that into your interior theme. This would also be wonderful with acorns added to it, sprayed gold or silver, and ribbons tied around, perhaps with candles. It could then function as a permanent altar dedicated to wisdom, strength, security, positivity, and intellect.

GROW AN OAK TREE

This might sound a bit ambitious, but you can do it in a number of ways. You might begin with a small pot, and put it on a balcony or terrace, beside a front door, or on a windowsill. You might ask your local government if they would let you plant one in a park; then you could visit it regularly and regard it as yours. You might ask a friend who has a garden to lend you space to "sponsor" an oak tree; or, you might just "adopt" one growing nearby in a park where you can go and sit under it, think around it, "breathe" it in. If all this really is impossible (if you haven't even got access to a park, for example), then paint an oak tree on a wall in your apartment, or even on a canvas, positioning it somewhere central in your home. TAKE ON THE STRENGTH OF AN OAK TREE, IN ANY WAY YOU CAN.

MAKING A PROTECTIVE RING AROUND YOUR HOUSE. One way of adding security to your life is to perform an overall protection spell to place in your home. This will have the effect of denying easy access to bad spirits and keeping you, as the dweller therein, optimistic. As with the birch ritual on pages 22-23, the circle is the most appropriate means of achieving this.

- If you are building a house from the ground up, put an acorn or oak leaf under the foundation stone, and say a prayer to the earth to protect you and the dwelling. Then walk once around the stone clockwise, and "charm" the earth under your feet with words of appreciation. Make them personal.

- When you move into a new house, and while it is still empty prior to your moving your furniture and possessions into the space, walk around each room in turn in a large clockwise circle, and sprinkle one of the oils listed on page 101 to secure the house for positivity. If you need to purify as well (for instance, if there has been an unhappy previous owner), sprinkle some rose oil in the circle, and place one red candle in the window on the first night.

- If your apartment is small, or you are already living there and just want to begin securing it now, make a circle of white lights with little votive candles in your main living area, and sit in the middle holding some oak, an acorn, a leaf—or even just a brown ribbon if you can't get anything oaky! Sprinkle the oil of one of your chosen scents (see page 101) in front of you, and breathe in a whole new state of being. Determine in your mind that life will begin to go smoothly, and that you will complete your projects, tasks, and goals with grace and strength. Keep the candles burning for about ten minutes while you visualize; then take each one to a different room and place a small flower beside it. Light each candle from time to time when you feel the need to rev up your positivity battery a little.

- If you are being really witchy, fill a bottle with some fresh earth (from a garden center, perhaps), place a lock of your hair in it, cork it, and wrap with a brick or brown and white ribbon. Walk once around the bottle in a circle, then encircle your own body with the bottle held at arm's length, and place it in a corner, either close to your hearth (if you have a fireplace) or perhaps near a potted plant. This recalls the ancient belief that a bad spirit had to count every grain of earth before taking up residence in a house. It would take a very long time to count the whole bottle, and the spirit might lose count several times and have to start again, so it would eventually give up!

- My own favorite method of drawing security and positivity into a dwelling (and a life) is to knot an old key—clock keys are wonderfully theatrical—with a piece of brown and white ribbon, looping in an acorn as well (pierce the acorn with a needle and thread string or thread through it). THIS LOOKS QUITE BEAUTIFUL, AND BOTH THE KEY AND THE ACORN ARE SYMBOLIC OF STRENGTH.

MASTER SPELL 1: TO DRAW FINANCIAL AND PERSONAL STRENGTH AND POSITIVITY.

This spell works very well to draw security, strength, and optimism into any area of your life. It might be required for financial certainty or as a general wish, or for a new relationship just getting off the ground which you want to progress with confidence and optimism.

YOU WILL NEED

A brick-red ribbon or cord; frankincense, sandalwood, or bay oil (or a blend of all three); a handful of oak leaves; your choice of candles; a crystal; a wooden or silver chalice filled with rainwater; 7 long stems of different-colored flowers (whatever is in season).

MOON PHASE: *Waxing*

Prepare by taking an oak bath. Tie the brick-red ribbon or cord around the faucets to "color" and power the water, and run the bath, adding 6–8 drops each of two or three of the oils at the end, and finally floating the oak leaves around the bath. Bathe by candlelight—the size, number, and color of the candles can be absolutely your own choice.

As you soak up the lovely leaves, envision exactly what it is that you hope for. Slide down into the water and close your eyes; see if you can "feel" a kind of force field around you, and visualize yourself victorious in your hopes within the power and light of this tremendous energy. Breathe in the oils, and say, *"Charge my spirit, cleanse my soul; Fill my life with happiness whole."* Take in the ideas and fill your senses from the eyes, the nose, the skin, the ears: THIS IS THE SWEET SMELL OF SUCCESS!

After your bath, sit in the candlelight and place the crystal into the rainwater-filled chalice, once again seeing security and continuance of all you hold dear—even an improvement in your affairs—but hold on tight to the one special thing you wish for.

If this concerns money and business, see steady success, rather than greedy piles of profit! Sure steps are what you are asking for. If your spell primarily concerns a relationship growing more secure, don't immediately expect commitments, but see a steady growth of communication, trust, interest, depth of feeling, and confidence. If you like, imagine you see all this in the ether of the light or in the crystal and chalice.

Finally, place the chalice (with the crystal inside) next to the flowers, and imagine all seven—the rainbow of colors—filling the cup with every shade of knowledge, growth, and strength. Untie the ribbon from the bathtub faucets, and place it around the chalice. Make a small, personally worded prayer for steady judgment and growing positivity.

Leave the items in place for 24 hours, and repeat the spell once more when the moon is again waxing—perhaps a month (or two) later. The power supply of positivity around you is now at its fullest!

MASTER SPELL 11: **TO AID FERTILITY.** This spell is also for use under the power of the oak moon. In high summer the earth is at its most pregnant, and petitions for personal fertility can be very effective at this time. If it seems just too wishful to imagine that a fertility spell will make you pregnant—especially if you've been trying for a while—just remember that many people agree that the mind, as well as the body, plays a part in conception, and that some women do get pregnant when the moment feels absolutely right. This spell is to help your body feel just that—and though it won't work miracles, it may push your mind-set into a higher gear.

YOU WILL NEED
Fertility herbs: cuttings of willow and oak, or acorns, seeds of parsley, cilantro, and Florence fennel; 1 white, 3 pink, and 3 blue candles.

MOON PHASE: *New.*

At sunset on a new moon during the summer period (but not necessarily at midsummer itself), plant any three of the above herbs in three patches to represent god, goddess, and earth, and father, mother, and child. Water in the seeds, asking for the great fecund earth to bring life to you and your partner, and as you sow the parsley—which germinates very slowly and is a symbol of patience regarding conception—imagine your own (or your partner's) body swelling with life and filled with green growth.

Mark each seed patch with a tiny candle (one each in blue, white, and pink), and trace a triangle in the earth. Four candles remain—two blue and two pink. Light these alternately over the four weeks following your seed planting, during which time you should get busy with your sexual contribution to fertility! AS THE SEEDS SPROUT, YOUR BODY SHOULD COME INTO ITS OWN CLOCK, AND IMAGINING SUCCESS MAY MAKE THE BIGGEST DIFFERENCE TO YOUR CHANCES OF CONCEIVING.

SUMMER

The earth is now lush with life at its most potent. As the oak moon ushers in summer, our own senses are brimming. Warm days entice smiles in the sun, a relaxed feeling, thoughts of vacations, and the wish to be outdoors. Now a witch's tasks are a pleasure: to plant a love garden rich with roses, violets, vervain, lavender, basil, lovage, and pansy; to create an altar in a high place; to pluck a magical rose at midsummer. This is also the appropriate moment for thinking of weddings—called handfasting ceremonies—which echo the marriage of the gods. In summer we may "conjure the stones" with a piece of crystal or fossil or a special gem. It is crucial, and delightful, to have a community celebration out of doors during this time. And now that you have learned how to mix incense, try the celebration incense for high summer, to capture the joy of the powerful sun. Element: fire. Direction: south.

THE SUMMER SOLSTICE: MIDSUMMER DAY. This day is the longest of the year, with total sunshine at the nearer pole. In the northern hemisphere this is around June 21st and in the south around December 21st.

In days past, it was traditional to stay up all night on Midsummer Eve waiting for the rising sun, to celebrate the longest day of the sun's powers. Bonfires were lit, and scented herbs and flowers, along with little ritual gifts, were burned as offerings. Celebrations often included torchlit processions and circles of revelers, with speeches to Fortuna, the lady of the wheel of fortune. The most important celebrations were held in circles of stone, where the sun was awaited for his magnificent heat and light from the earliest dawn. Marriages were performed at this time between couples who had pledged their unison at Imbolc or Beltane (May Day). Jumping over fires or wafting smoke was a sign of purification and sharing the sun's power.

Witches now work to capture the power of the sun. Evolve your own ritual with a mirror and a white candle—white being the color of midsummer. Mirrors are sacred in magic for their intense reflective powers and because they capture symbolically the image of the ethereal light source. A ritual might include making a wish on a high place, with a candle and a mirror glinting with the sun's light. Take time to notice and enjoy the day. Always make wishes for others, too, who need help in something. Leave a nosegay of simple summer flowers tied with ribbon on the summit after the wish, as an offering to the god and goddess who are symbolically married at high summer. This is why marriage is perfect for us at this time.

The Summer Solstice is the peak moment for working magic ritual with standing stones, as at Stonehenge or Avebury, in England. If you have none, you could create a mini stone circle in your garden. Fill a cauldron with fresh flowers and water for a summer ritual, within the stone circle if possible. Most importantly, share the day with good friends and have fun, for this is the spirit of the solstice.

MIDSUMMER FEAST

The celebration of midsummer assists the earth—now pregnant—to carry well and bear a fruitful crop. There is a correlation between this idea and all the magical concepts of the chapter for security, positivity, and success. This is the moment to light the fires of protection and see a sound conclusion to a job well done in the months ahead.

Simple celebrations abound. You might honor the oak—and in conjunction, security and dependability—by tying a ribbon (not yellow) around an old oak tree. Kiss the tree as you do so, and thank the earth for your home. Promise to be more aware of others who need little blessings in any shape or form.

Set trestle tables out of doors at midsummer, and honor the beautiful, resilient, wise earth. See yourself within its vibration: as a breeze blows, think how it affects you. Invite friends to the feast, asking each to bring a plate of outdoor food. Always include some herb-based treat: I like to serve sorrel tartlets, or lavender-flavored meats. Have a choice of desserts that celebrate the fruit harvests of summer: berries of all types. Wines, equally, might be rather unusual, based on flowers or berries instead of the grape. And do have some music, of any kind: this honors vibratory positivity in a unique way.

CONJURING THE STONES. Stones have a special place in ritual and magic. Huge menhirs were placed for ritual in the great stone henges of our ancestors, and gemstones have been thought lucky and powerful for individual use in most cultures. Rocks and stones have knowledge of the earth and the past and the great climactic changes that took place long ago. When we borrow from their energies, we borrow from their wisdom and survival. In the Italian tradition of witchcraft, a stone found with any kind of hole in it was thought especially lucky, a mark of favor from the moon goddess Diana.

When you find a stone in summer, either on the beach, on the road, or simply in a shop, pay attention to it and mark it with this ritual to empower the stone and align it with your own energies. Say: "*I have found upon my path today this holy-stone (originally a stone with a hole); I thank thee, Lady, for this lucky present, and the spirit which left it for me here; I charge it by the sun's great light to bring me luck and give me strength in adversity.*" (At this, show it to the sun, and look through the hole at the sunlight.)

Later on that same day at night, say: "*Tonight, by the moon's ethereal light, I charge it to bring me great fortune and deep thought. May its magnetic strengths give me the knowledge to draw to me those things that make my life complete.*" The following morning, rise a shade earlier than usual and say, holding the stone: "*I rise in the early dawn, and through vales and meadows fair, or in towns and past houses, I walk with luck and knowledge to endure. All decisions I shall make now shall be wise. All friendships I make shall be strong. All paths I seek shall open to me.*"

Now throw the stone up to the heavens three times and catch it, then finish: "*I beg of thee, good spirit of the Lady, enter this stone and rest here in my pocket.*" Always keep the stone in a safe place.

Your stone is now signature to you and magical, and will bring you strange proofs of luck. Use it in ceremony, wisely and not greedily, and thank the spirit of the Lady when you are granted your desires. Any stone found in summer is a holy-stone, and especially those with a hole in them, or that are completely rounded. If you are given a gem in high summer, you may wish to dedicate it in this same way.

A SUMMER LOVE GARDEN. At the start of summer lay out a garden celebrating the power of love. It doesn't matter how small your potential garden space is— even if you have only a little window box or tub, you can grow any of the following flowers to attract love and to perform love magic.

If you have been attentive, you will have sown seeds in preparation for this in spring and will now have seedlings ready; otherwise you can buy established plants.

Lavender is easy to grow and will be your best friend for love pouches and sachets, as well as a healing plant. Varieties come in blue, mauve, pink, and white in all sizes. If you have room for only one plant, make it lavender. A rose bush is essential, even if it must be a miniature. For love, choose pink and deep red shades, but always opt for scent. If you have space, old varieties in shrub form are indispensable for love spells and love potions. Delicate violets smell fabulous and attract love vibrations right to where you live; they have a short flowering season, but can be crystallized successfully. One tiny pot will provide hours of pleasure and a delightfully potent ingredient for potpourris and especially love elixirs. As you tend your roses and violets, dedicate them to Juno and Venus, the goddesses of female strength, allure, and wisdom—you will have powerful allies.

Basil, lemon balm, and rosemary will attract love to the grower and are potent ingredients in magical spells. And lastly, if you have space, sow borage and/or sweet peas—life will never be dull with these magical flowers around you.

Plant your herbs and flowers in a pretty shape: a heart, a crescent moon, or a star will all add to the magic and will bring you astounding luck in your life—especially in love. If you desire fairy activity in the garden, place some crystals among the plants. I love to put little ribbons in between the flowers to bring rainbow happiness into the garden. Pots can also be tied with ribbons: pink to bring general love, red for passion, blue for loyalty. Harvest the flowers when they are in full bloom, and either dry them for potpourris or put them in glass jars for later use. Roses, lavender, and sweet peas will scent sugar deliciously, and you can then cook up love dishes with their fragrance.

FLOWERS AND HERBS WITH MAGICAL PROPERTIES. Here is a guide to what you can do with the flowers you harvest during late spring and summer. Because summer sees the goddess at her marriage, I have concentrated on flowers and herbs with special beauty options.

SWEET VIOLET The beautiful scented flowers of this delicate little plant, white and mauve colored, appear from late winter to very late spring. The scent whispers mystery but also innocence. So powerful is the fragrance that smelling the flower directly is possible only for a few seconds, after which the olfactory senses shut down for a rest and start again a moment later! The flower syrup treats coughs, headaches, and insomnia—good for the night before an important day. The dried aerial parts of the plant also treat eczema and skin eruptions. Sweet violet was a well-known cordial for the heart and a principal ingredient in many love potions. Try it in wine.

LINDEN OR LIME BLOSSOM Here we have an untapped joy. It has a wonderful "green," grassy fragrance, and is a fabulous tonic for scalp, nails, and hair. Like violet, it treats nervous headache and tension as well as insomnia and is good for fractious children—try a mild tea. Cosmetically it has excellent properties for sensitive skin and is wonderful in a bath for muscular aches and pains. Men enjoy its honest fragrance, too. It has the smell of a florist's shop.

LILAC This is one of my absolute favorites. The scent is intense, rich, sweet, and warm; one shrub can perfume the whole summer garden. Flower colors are particularly varied—mauve, purple, white, and pink. The florets make a wonderful dessert garnish in food (try them just on ice cream), and the flowers and leaves cheer up a potpourri. There is a close connection with lilacs as a *"fairy flower."* In simple bowls or vases, they make one feel fey, ethereal, and enigmatic—have them by when meeting a loved one.

ELDERFLOWER It is harder now to find these flowers on country walks than it used to be, because so many are gathered to make the popular homemade cordial. Elderflower has an unusual green scent that would blend well with other florals in a vase for a love altar. As a light tea, it aids hay fever sufferers before the worst of the season, and the cooled tea also treats sore or tired eyes and an inflamed face—excellent for boys as an aftershave. Magically, you need the support of the elder mother to be bewitching, so respect the flowers.

ROSE GERANIUM Here is a scent that is well known now, but the plant has some fabulous properties that are not so well understood. It releases its characteristic rosy-green smell, which makes it a favorite for perfumes and potpourris. Victorian skirts brushed against the leaves to release their scent. The essential oil is tonic, antiseptic, and antidepressant and treats sluggish systems, cellulite, poor circulation, and unbalanced skin. A drop or two in the bath refreshes and rejuvenates. It also magically protects against negative thoughts from others. Try some leaves in cooking.

EVENING PRIMROSE Known to many for its powers of restoration after a heavy night-before, this is a wonderful hangover cure. We know what it does for menopausal or premenstrual tension, but in capsule form it also helps to reduce eczema and feed healthy skin. The flowers have a sweet honey scent and are magically very associated with women in control. Grow some in a pot—just to make you smile.

HONEYSUCKLE A fragrant climber that is quite lovely and worth including, even though it takes space to grow. The scent from its beautiful creamy yellow and pink flowers wafts through summer gardens, providing a mesmeric haven for humming bees on summer nights. The whole scent and headiness of the honeysuckle has been associated forever with romance and tenacity in love. The flowers (also called woodbine) yield a skin-softening toilet water with a powerful, trademark scent. The oil is quite expensive but is prized for cosmetic use, especially if the real thing (rather than a synthetic) is used. The twining flowers magically speak of loyalty in a relationship.

GARDENIA This is another of my favorites and surprisingly, it is easy to grow in a small pot on a windowsill. This talented and exotic flower treats nosebleeds, toothache, and skin sores. The scent is balanced, like lavender and carnation—all have a perfect high, middle, and low note. It is needed only, therefore, as a single floral note. Simply float the exotic blooms in warm water to release their sensuous fragrance, or place a pot close at hand for a romantic summer evening supper.

ORRIS OR IRIS Where to begin? This is a floral wonder and forms a magical ingredient in face packs, scented sachets, shampoos, body powders, and even tooth powders. It has a complex violet scent, used in soaps and perfumes. Iris was the flower of the goddess of the rainbow: in magic, a stem is synonymous with peace and feminine powers of persuasion.

BASIL This lush-leafed and tasty plant is a favorite pot herb; it comes in rainbow colors, too. Its green leaves are best known, but purple and variegated varieties are interesting alternatives, and the leaves of some varieties are lemon-scented. All are deliciously pungent when crushed in hot sun; the leaves steeped in wine are renowned as a tonic and aphrodisiac (sometimes one and the same thing). It is a top-note oil, with a sunny, "light-green" fragrance, used as a smelling salt to revive our over-corseted female ancestors. Also antiseptic, tonic, and a stimulant, the scent alone goads the tired brain into a flurry of focused ability; diluted oil or a very strong tea can be excellent as a footbath for summer feet. It should not be used during pregnancy. In Italy it is regarded magically as sacred to attracting love.

ROSES Ubiquitous in magic, these wonderfully sweet-scented flowers arrived, according to legend, with the birth of Venus, or Aphrodite, goddess of love. Magically, rose attracts love and protects lovers. It should be used in quantity to nurture a new love and equally to perpetuate a seasoned love affair. Always smell rose when you're under stress, or feeling emotional burnout, overwork, or any worries concerned with femininity. The goddess of the garden, its blooms in a vase are as magical as its petals in a glass of summer wine. Rosewater is inestimable as a gentle, soothing wash for tired skin, and good for people who are sensitive to many other products. It was used to fragrance the hair and put the goddess's own hand protectively on the heads of maidens courting love. Used after surgery, rose skin creams will speed healing. Rose works well for purification, to treat someone suffering from negative feelings, self-doubt, or emotional disappointment. The cream is perfectly suited to treating drier or older skins, but sensitive skins also flourish on it. (See page 118 for a special summer rose ritual.)

JASMINE This exotic immigrant needs no introduction. Its powerful, erotic fragrance is the favorite in many eastern countries. On warm evenings, the clusters of flowers on its elegant fronds emit a warm, narcotic scent. In love magic, jasmine was used in self-hypnosis to help the wearer assume greater powers of confidence and control than they might otherwise feel. The flowers may be tied into the hair for scent. The oil is very expensive, but a little goes a very long way. Cosmetically it helps dry, sensitive skins and corrects tiredness and is the best on offer for helping to overcome anxieties of a sexual nature. Not to be used at all in pregnancy, it is nevertheless excellent diluted as a massage oil during the birth itself.

MADONNA LILY This fabulous fragrance is justly famous, and less sickly than other lilies. The flower yields an essential oil which is prized for perfume, and the summer bulbs have excellent cosmetic properties, particularly for ointments and for treating sunburned or inflamed skins. The distilled flower water, like rose and lavender water and orange blossom water, is a wonderful skin toner. When infused with almond oil, it makes an excellent massage oil and counters eczema.

TUBEROSE This truly exotic plant has lily-white flowers with an unbelievably intense, narcotic, sensuous fragrance. It is one of the most expensive scents and oils in the world and its sensuous scent frees up recalcitrant lovers. Tuberose was so sacred it was used to fragrance the cool marble interiors of Italian basilicas. In Mexico, it is used to enhance the flavor of chocolate. Use in open spaces.

LAVENDER If it were only possible to grow one magical plant, this would be it. Among its myriad attributes is the power to bestow sensuality, clarity, confidence, and humor, all of which qualities are induced as we inhale the perfume of this lovely plant. A sweet, cleansing, but also relaxing fragrance, it is, like rose, the principal scent for potpourris, drawer liners, herb pillows, incense burners, and dried flower bunches. A healthful drink and culinary aid, lavender cures insomnia, headaches, and nausea and even eases halitosis as a mouthwash. Lavender water tones the face, aids in cell renewal, and treats acne. Magically, it is connected with overcoming depression or nervousness in love. It is associated with the bewitching powers of a woman—particularly women in their later twenties and over, who are no longer "green" in love!

A MIDSUMMER NIGHT'S ROSE. This ancient ritual has fulfilled the romantic dreams of countless young girls. Why not try it yourself?

YOU WILL NEED

A white rose (picked as below); a sheet of white tissue paper; a white shoe box.

On the Summer Solstice, at the chime of midnight, go silently into the garden and pick a white rose. (If you don't have a garden or space outside, you may have to cheat a little and find one.) Remember, this whole ritual must be done without speaking a word to anyone. Clasp the rose to your bosom, and make a wish for happiness in love. Now walk silently backward indoors and wrap the rose carefully in some clean, white tissue paper. Place it in a white shoe box, and set it aside safely until Yule, or, if you prefer, Christmas Day. On that day wear the rose pinned to your outfit (preferably a white top), and on that very day you should have a declaration of love.

A LAVENDER RITUAL. On long, lazy, summery days, when you have a headache that simply won't go away, a loved one is trying to tell you something! Try this ritual with lavender sprigs, preferably fresh from your own garden or pot (but dried will do).

YOU WILL NEED

1 tablespoon fresh lavender leaves (1 teaspoon dried); 2¹/₂ cups boiling water; ¹/₂ teaspoon honey.

Make a mild infusion of lavender tea, and sweeten it with honey. Brew for ten minutes, then sip the tea slowly, preferably outside. While you are drinking, ask who is thinking of you and what they wish to say to you. Look into the cup, and you should soon see the face of your love, or someone else who is thinking of you. While you drink your tea, the message will come through, and your headache will evaporate.

THE HANDFASTING CEREMONY. The Pagan form of marriage should ideally take place as a dual event unfolding around May 1st (for the proposal or declaration of feeling, privately and then publicly) and culminating in a high-summer handfasting ceremony, traditionally around the Summer Solstice itself. This echoes the perceived marriage of the god and goddess and has long influenced the popularity of a June wedding.

Handfasting is the witches' variation of a marriage ceremony. It will be recognized legally only if officiated over by a celebrant or officer with the power to conduct such legal ceremonies in that vicinity. The pledge is to last "a year and a day," to be renewed on the same date twelve months hence. A year and a day will preserve the original date rather than the day of the week, which is why all our anniversaries move from a Monday to a Tuesday the following year, and so on.

The date is more important than the day, so choose it with care; but the original day of the week is also important, as it carries the original spirit and luck, setting things in motion. So think about this, too, when you choose your day for the ceremony. Oddly enough, Saturday, which is the most popular day for Christian or secular weddings, is probably the least lucky day! Try instead to choose a Friday, which is dedicated to Venus; or a Wednesday, when you have Woden with you. Usually the couples join their right hands, hand to hand, to symbolize their rational, male side; they then join left hands, joining their intuitive/female selves. Seen overall, with both hands crossed over each other, this makes the symbol of infinity. Both parties may choose words that have individual resonance. Orange blossom, lilac blossom, or rose petals should be strewn over the couple by friends, both as purification and as a magnet for strength in love and adversity. At the culmination, some couples may choose to "jump over a broom" into the realms of marriage—but don't worry; this can be omitted if it feels odd.

Handfasting should be followed by a feast that includes the consumption of orange and of honey; so invite friends together if you are ready to make or renew these vows. June is the traditional month for handfasting, as it is the month of the oak, representing firmness of heart. The couple should be given a planted baby oak tree as a symbol of their union.

INCENSE AND MARRIAGE

Sweetly scented smoke spiraling upward ritually honors the power of the sun. Fire is involved in so much ritual, and incense is a simple way to bring this element into your magic. Both scent and vibration are released into the ether to carry thought. Nothing is more powerful for a ceremony of love, such as marriage (or handfasting), as the smoke sends a message of serious intent to the heavens. It purifies and attracts the best spirit.

High summer incense could include orange blossom, orange peel, orange essential oil, frankincense (sacred to the sun), and rose petals; it is sacred to marriage, honoring the union of goddess and god. Mix it on a Friday, also sacred to love. This incense is best burned on a charcoal burner and wafted through the area for love.

ENCIRCLEMENT

HOLLY MOON

THERE

ARE TIMES WHEN ONE LONGS TO BE ABLE

TO TURN THE CLOCK BACK. THIS CHAPTER IS ABOUT

REVERSING DIFFICULT SITUATIONS—WE LEARN THE MAGIC

REQUIRED TO REVERSE A PROBLEMATIC SITUATION THAT IS STILL VIABLE.

UNHAPPY WORDS AND TENSE RELATIONSHIPS CAN BE "UNWISHED" OR "UN-SAID"

BY CHANGING THEIR "POLARITY"; RESCUES CAN OCCUR (METAPHORICALLY) EVEN

BEFORE A SITUATION HAS REACHED THE POINT OF HARMFUL IMPACT. IF THERE IS A

BUSINESS THREAT OR A HEALTH PROBLEM ARISING, OR EVEN A DIFFICULTY STARTING TO

AFFECT A LOVE RELATIONSHIP, THE HOLLY MOON IS THE ONE THAT CAN GOVERN TURNING

THINGS AROUND 180 DEGREES. THIS EVEN STRETCHES TO INCLUDE A SPELL AGAINST

GOSSIPING! THIS SUMMER MOON INCLUDES THE SABBAT OF LUGHNASADH (OR LAMMAS)

ON AUGUST 1–2, A GRAIN FESTIVAL; MAKING FLOWER DOLLS AND CORN DOLLS IS PART

OF THE MAGIC ELEMENT OF HONORING THIS TIME. THE HOLLY MOON—THE

MOON OF POLARITY—COVERS THE PERIOD EARLY JULY TO EARLY AUGUST.

IT IS THE REVERSAL OF SUMMER, THE DAYS LEADING INEXORABLY

TOWARD WINTER AND THE MOMENT OF THE HOLLY

KING, ONE MODEL FOR SANTA CLAUS.

LAMMAS: THE FEAST OF HIGH SUMMER. The Pagan festival of Lammas is a celebration of the first fruits of the harvest—an early crop. The word itself derives from "Hlafmas," an Anglo-Saxon word which translates as the "loaf mass." This refers to the importance of the grain, and is a celebration of the first picking of wheat. In the Irish tradition, the god Lugh is associated with this festival, and the day called Lughnasadh. It is a Celtic moon festival, and can be recognized even in the Roman moon goddess, Luna.

Great magic made now must be for career success, prosperity, material resolutions, and protection. Be generous, but pay back debts. Drawing on old magic, place a corn doll in the garden (or on your desk) to ensure protection from storms. (This translates to us as the placing of a lucky doll-object to ensure safe haven; it is still a custom to throw a doll of herbs or corn [wheat] into floodwaters to encourage them to abate.) These storms may be metaphoric—the weathering of pressure at work, or difficulty in deciding what to do vocationally. Cast your thoughts out on the tide with a small herb-crafted doll to attract powerful insights and to manifest directions from nature and the gods.

If a business or commercial idea is launched now, buy or make a charm-doll, dedicated to the goddess, to keep away problems and invite success. Visit a sacred well or river to carry your spirits into the realm of action rather than thought, and to effect healing or rest. Float flowers and herbs tied into a shape in a fast-running river, asking for help and the creation of a signpost or direction for your future.

On a social level, Lammas is the time to bake bread and invite friends for a wish party. Birthday cake celebrations derive from this—but the bread should be broken rather than cut. Crumbs should be tossed to the birds for luck and to thank the god and goddess for providing. If it is a brilliant sunny day, take a long walk and mark the day properly. Make some connection with grains (any grain, even pasta, noodles, or couscous) when making your evening meal.

The key aspects of the celebration are concerned with corn dolls, grain ales, and the waning moon, as well as the idea of a buried treasure in the earth! As the grain is harvested, so the earth's progeny dies; implicit in this death, however, is the polar concept that in spring all will be reborn.

To make good earth magic and to bless your own workings over the course of the coming winter days, ensuring re-emergence into sunshine and fecundity again, work with friends to bake special loaves of unusual breads which will recognize the importance of this simple grain. If you have a taste for whisky, which was traditional and sacred to this festival, try sampling something special and toasting the friends around you. Make wishes as you sip! Otherwise, if beers are more pleasing to your palate, make an informal feast out of corn chips and a few glasses of your favorite brew.

HOLLY MOON—MOON OF ENCIRCLEMENT AND POLARITY. Color: BRONZE, SUNSHINE YELLOW. Scent: CILANTRO, TUBEROSE, BENZOIN. Number: 8.

There comes a moment when, no matter how much positive magic you have worked toward any one situation, life and events seem destined to take their own course and career down a path that is out of your control.

"O! Call back yesterday, bid time return."
RICHARD II, ACT 3 SCENE II
WILLIAM SHAKESPEARE

Perhaps in a relationship, despite careful tending and real effort, an inevitable misunderstanding or flash of careless anger threatens to dismantle everything you have worked for. Perhaps a business, which you have nurtured, now shows signs of fatigue; or another goal in business or your career which you have been steadily moving toward suddenly appears to be out of reach or beyond your hopes. This is the moment to work "polarity magic."

Polarity can also be seen as a rebalancing: a situation has gone too far in one direction and must be brought back the other way. As with all magic, some of this can be done with the deft use of physical ingredients (oils, herbs, and colors), while much of it is achieved through the powerful concentration of the mind, which exerts a dedicated magnetic pull to draw a situation gently back from its current (errant!) position. You must believe with all your might that you can effect this response.

HOLLY

A sprig of holly, or a holly leaf, makes a talisman with a similar effect to that of a magnet; however, it is a better choice if the reversal you want to achieve concerns sharp words that have passed between you and a lover, friend, employer, family member, or whomever. Place a photograph of yourself and the wounded (or offended) party on a small table, or in a little box or basket, surrounded by eight holly leaves. Meanwhile, burn a bronze or yellow candle nearby, and gently say that you are sorry for your own part in the misunderstanding or argument that has befallen you both. Ask for tolerance and a chance to set things right.

If the situation is really serious, and you are involved in a breakup, try planting both a male and a female holly tree, side by side, someplace where you can attend to them. If you don't have a yard yourself, sponsor the trees in a friend's yard! As you plant them, place each of your names in the dug-out holes. Say a loving benediction, and tend the trees warmly.

THE SCENTS AND COLORS OF REBALANCE

Part of polarity magic is the ability to realize that a situation is under threat and to arrest it before it disappears irrevocably down a terminal path!

This may sound silly, but pause for a moment: if you can honestly assess a tricky relationship, or identify a potential cause of angry disagreement before it has deteriorated into intransigent behavior on both sides, you should be able to express disquiet or confusion without malice and insecurity, and avoid a serious problem. To achieve this equanimity, you need to breathe in the scents of balance, which effectively encourage you to try to see some of the problem from the other party's point of view. After all, the chances are that there are two sides to the quarrel or situation that has brought you to anger.

Surround yourself with a circle of eight candles, bronze-yellow in color, and with the use of an oil burner, breathe in tuberose oil, or benzoin, or geranium, or a mixture of the three. Ask yourself how a secure and balanced person, no longer in the first flush of wrath, would deal with this issue: can you find a steady, nonexplosive way of framing your questions, and be reasonable about it? Once you have seen some way forward, take the scents with you to the meeting, or burn them while you are speaking to the other party on the telephone. A disaster could thereby be averted, and you will encourage the other person also to rebalance their viewpoint, and see the justness of your position.

If you are dealing with a person or people who are perpetually quick to anger, try sprinkling these rebalancing oils around the "arena" before you all meet. If an argument has already occurred and you need to patch things up, write the names of the parties involved on good-quality paper, saturate the page with one of the oils, and tie it into a little scroll secured with yellow ribbon and—if you can get it—gold sealing wax.

Send the mental message of peace and forgiveness with the act. Apologies will then be able to take place gently.

LETTING GO

Perhaps a quarrel has developed, and it is not the first time. The rebalancing that you have in mind is to release the anger and pain, and then to reverse your own feelings of emotion so that you can effectively move on. Consult the chapter on DISENCHANTMENT (pages 88-97), but work some of the following advice in with your magic.

Surround yourself with sunflowers, or use a mandrake if you can get one! Burn the oils of rebalance, and use a magnet to envision a reversal of the existing situation that has been making you unhappy. Now write your name on a piece of paper, and next to it write the name of the party who has caused you grief or distress. Tie up a holly leaf with the paper, using yellow cord, and place the whole in a little plastic container. Cover with honey, then add a good pinch of salt. This shows a willingness to pour salt into the wound—but also to add honey which will heal it!

OTHER SYMBOLS YOU COULD UTILIZE FOR LETTING GO:

- A CLOCK RUNNING BACKWARD (to show time being reversed), and ribbons that are actually untied. Use these items with a photo either to let go yourself or to move the relationship back in time to the point of combustion. Then, re-imagine the ending you want as vividly as you can!

- A SEMICIRCLE (180 degrees), which is excellent for business magic. If money has been running out, pin a protractor to a dollar bill, and tie it with gold cord. Imagine everything running forward, healthy and positive.

COUNTERACTIVE MAGIC. It may be that your life has now reached a moment when you want to turn everything around and begin to travel in the opposite direction. This kind of magic should creep into everyday life; it is prescribed when, for example, every relationship you have had seems to have ended in disappointment or failure.

If, perpetually, you begin a love affair with someone and everything is going well, only to suddenly and inexplicably enter a bad patch and end, you need to work polarity magic. Maybe you always reach a point where you believe things must go wrong—because they always have in the past! It is time to turn the clock around and go the other way.

This can be just as true in your business, career, or working life. Perhaps you have always reached a particular point and then failed to make the very highest grade because you said something tactless, or maybe you simply don't feel secure enough to push yourself forward any further. You must see yourself as a success, and dispel the feeling of being doomed to repeated failure. Indeed, if you have any repetition of events that you would like to change—lapses into arguments with friends and in-laws, perhaps, or bad luck, or even ongoing ailments with the same theme (like repeated colds)—you need to work on the magnetic opposite.

COUNTERACTIVE MAGIC IN EVERYDAY LIFE

If you need to arrest a downward slide in any area of your life, you must work very hard to turn things around mentally. This amounts to a kind of psychological reconditioning: but this is partly what magic is about.

Begin by cleansing your environment. Spin a nest of bright yellow or bronze-sunshine colored light around the room(s) in your mind's eye, first in a clockwise direction, then counterclockwise, to show an "unwinding" of what has gone before. Place a small magnet in the room.

Scent the room(s) with coriander and benzoin oils, and add a drop or two of tuberose if you have it. These oils are associated with transformation, balance, and self-forgiveness—the last of which is sometimes the easiest to overlook when you need to overcome a negative spiral. If matters continually seem to degenerate, or you feel you have messed up an otherwise good situation, it is essential to forgive yourself and move on.

COMPASS

A compass (with cardinal points) is a symbol associated with the desire to change direction in a situation. If this emblem appeals to you, try writing a letter of apology to someone you have fallen out with and enclose a compass in the envelope to signify a new wind blowing through your minds, ushering you both to calmer climes. Or, perhaps you wish to turn around a business that is floundering or an academic course that is not going the way you would like it to. Firstly, you must cleanly envision a new, more positive direction emerging in your business or study life; then, taking some appropriate paperwork, put a beautiful compass into a folder with the papers and tie them up with a yellow ribbon. As you do this, visualize a change: see negativity replaced with positive results.

MASTER SPELL: TO REVERSE A DIFFICULT SITUATION. This spell will help you to turn back the clock—with either a situation you wish had never started or one that may have started to deteriorate. It should erase negative feelings and insecurity.

YOU WILL NEED

A photo of the person with whom you have reached a stalemate, if relevant, or documents (such as a letter, note, lawsuit, or bank statement) that pertain to the impasse; a small mirror (no more than 8 x 10 inches) with a bronze or yellow frame; 8 sunshine-yellow votive candles; a small horseshoe-shaped magnet wrapped in yellow cord or ribbon; a large sunflower.

MOON PHASE: *Waning*

Before you begin, focus for a very long time on the documents, or photo, and what they represent; try to think very calmly about the difficulty of the situation, but do not allow yourself to see it as irrevocable, even for a second.

Place the documents, or photo, on a table in front of the mirror, and light the candles. Breathe deeply, and be quiet and still. Retrace in your mind all the steps that led up to the current problem—but stop short of the actual disaster, quarrel, or let-down. If you can now perceive the one bad move that led to the present state of affairs, start to visualize strongly a large clockface, with the hands turning backward, and possibly even a calendar flipping back until you arrive at the day or hour when everything went wrong.

Now grasp the magnet in your hands, turn it toward the mirror and documents or photo, and draw in the light from the candle flames. Strongly envision the events immediately prior to the bad moment, and then vividly rewrite the outcome in your mind. Imagine that the conversation took a different direction, or that spiky words, or a negative reply, which came in place of something positive you had hoped for, are now replaced by a gentle, harmonious conclusion. Be bold in your mind, but avoid being pushy in what you wish to see occur; rather, see a gentle retraction of the negativity or unhappiness that occurred. See a much happier end to the whole episode. Focus on this thought, quietly, for several moments; imagine the face of the other person or people involved, and see yourself departing from them in a positive way. Circle them with light in your imagination; say "sorry," if necessary.

Loop the magnet into the documents or photo, and secure with yellow cord or ribbon. Place a sunny sunflower, symbol of hope, in front of the mirror where the papers or photo lay before—replacing sadness with brightness. Put the magnet and papers or photo into an envelope or box, and file them somewhere right away. Let the candles burn down in front of the mirror, and every so often revisit them, and imagine the happier conclusion again for a few minutes.

After no more than a week, if appropriate, reopen communications or contact the person—if they have not already approached you with the same goal in mind. If it is in your best interests, it should now be possible to repair the damage.

WISDOM

HAZEL MOON

CHAPTER CENTERS ON THE CRONE MOON,

OR MOON OF THE WISE, AND TAKES THE ACQUISITION OF

KNOWLEDGE AND ALL MATTERS OF EDUCATION TO ITS HEART. THIS

MAGIC CONCERNS ANYONE STUDYING, TAKING AN EXAM, TRYING TO TAKE IN

INFORMATION. WITHOUT BEING TOO GRAND, IT ALSO COVERS DRIVING TESTS AND

COOKING COURSES! FROM EARLY AUGUST TO THE BEGINNING OF SEPTEMBER—THE

PERIOD COVERED BY THE HAZEL MOON—WE ARE WITNESSING THE LATE POWER OF THE

SUN; THIS IS A HEYDAY PERIOD: A MOMENT FOR REFLECTION AND HEIGHTENED AWARENESS.

THERE IS NO PARTICULAR CELEBRATION DAY WITHIN THIS MOON/MONTH. HOWEVER, WE

CAN ENJOY A PROLONGED HARVEST FESTIVAL RIGHT THROUGH THE PERIOD, FROM THE

PREVIOUS HOLLY MOON UNTIL THE VINE MOON OF CELEBRATION (PAGES 144-157); THIS

COINCIDES WELL WITH THE ENGLISH CHURCH'S HARVEST FESTIVAL. A "GOOD WITCH"

STRIVES TO KNOW WHEN IT IS VALID, AND WHEN INVALID, TO TACKLE ANY TASK

IN MAGIC—OR, PUT ANOTHER WAY, WHEN NOT TO DO OR UNDO

SOMETHING. THERE ARE ALWAYS TIMES WHEN IT IS BEST TO LEAVE

HAZEL MOON—MOON OF WISDOM. Colors: OLIVE GREEN, MULBERRY. Scents: HYACINTH, ROSE ATTAR (for forgiveness), ROSEMARY, SANDALWOOD, LAVENDER (for the mind). Number: 9. Now we set out to acquire wisdom.

"One impulse from a vernal wood
  May teach you more of man;
  Of moral evil and of good
  Than all the sages can."
"THE TABLES TURNED"
  WILLIAM WORDSWORTH

You have come thus far down the road, and are starting to grasp the mental elasticity required for good magic and to embrace very subtly the philosophy behind Wicca thinking. At this stage you must put your reflective powers into action, and start to make a difference, not only to your own life but also to those around you.

The hazel is the tree long held to be symbolic of the acquisition of knowledge and philosophy, but rather unusually, two other trees are associated with this moon cycle, owing to their long connection with wisdom, forgiveness, and spiritual understanding. The first of these is the mulberry, which refuses to put out any sign of growth until all danger of frost is past, and the second is the olive tree, which is sometimes one of the core thirteen trees, notably in the French Celtic tradition. The olive is, of course, associated with peace.

Hazel is one of the few witches' trees that were not valued primarily for their medicinal properties. Although it does have applications in medicine, its principal value comes from the use that can be made of its wood, its oil, and the nutritious nuts that it bears. The wood has long been used for walking sticks and rods (symbols of wisdom), as well as in the making of hurdle fences and wattles (the underlying framework in the walls of some medieval houses). Significantly, it is one of the main woods used to make divining rods (along with willow, or withy). Only someone wise, skilled, and patient could dowse—and indeed, to this day the job of diviner is often hereditary. Perhaps this is the first connection between the tree and wisdom.

Besides this, hazel nuts and oil are highly nutritious and might well be regarded as "brain food"—rich as they are in fat and protein. In the past, the oil was used not only in cooking (as now) but also to make soaps and cosmetics. In magic, this valuable oil is often used in ritual.

Mulberry is a byword for medicinal wisdom in China and has been cultivated for its beneficial properties since it was brought to Europe from the Middle East at the time of the Crusades. It is famously used as a food for silkworms, but the fruits are valued as diuretics and in the treatment of painful periods and diarrhea.

It is fascinating that the seventeenth-century herbalist Nicholas Culpeper lists both the hazel and the mulberry as ruled by Mercury, who is associated with wisdom and the hazel rod of knowledge. Inherent in this, the ninth moon, is the power of the number 9. This number embraces the philosophy of full knowledge; it is the last number of the ordinary cycle, 1 to 9, and assumes familiarity with all the numerological ideas that have passed before. As such it represents wisdom, forgiveness, wide reading, travel, and a humanitarian understanding of our fellow creatures—both human and animal.

THE MAGIC OF WISDOM IN EVERYDAY LIFE

The magic concerning wisdom is contemplative. It is important to recognize that we know very little straight off the top of our heads: or rather, whereas the initial impact of any given information will certainly touch off an intuitive response, it is the considered, well-rounded, patient conclusion we reach after some reflection that is the most reliable guide to our appropriate behavior and reaction in any situation. This moon reminds us not to "fly off the handle;" it exemplifies the pleasure and depth that come to us from learning and reading later in life, in place of the first rush of enthusiasm, at best—and outright reluctance, at worst—that we feel toward learning in the earlier part of our lives. This moon is about the fruits of a little experience!

To turn up our capacity for receptiveness and open our minds to new information—instead of closing ourselves off to what is unfamiliar—certain colors, symbols, and scents spark off a more relaxed and inquiring state of mind. And here, for the first time as an essential, music plays a vital part in our developing brain. It is a belief seemingly common to all religious philosophy that "the music of the spheres" and chanting deepen our concentration and stimulate the mind to receive wisdom.

TRIGGERING MEMORY AND BRAIN ACTIVITY DAILY

- One way to step up your mental powers is to cover school books and work files in mulberry and/or olive colors, and scent the paperwork with a little of one of the oils listed on page 138. Or place scented handkerchiefs in your drawers, so that a little therapeutic aroma escapes as you work away, enticing your mind to stay fresh.

- Place a tissue imbued with the scents described on page 138, or a sachet of fresh rosemary and lavender, in your pencil case or disk box so that your mind is firing, but calmly, as you embark on work and education.

- Take a leaf out of a medieval book, and strew herbs around your floor, or tie bunches around the study or office—again, make rosemary, lavender, and basil your principal choices.

- If you want to breathe in mental alertness—or an atmosphere of wise restraint—in the place where you work, grow one huge tub of herbs which includes rosemary, lavender, basil, and thyme, and even a small lemon tree if conditions allow. Stroking the leaves regularly, or before an important occasion, will release the right aromatic "buzz" into the room.

DOWSING

Begin on your path toward joining the adept by fashioning yourself a hazel rod (at last—a magic wand is prescribed!). Remember that it is symbolic of the tree of knowledge; if you can learn to use it to dowse, all the better.

Dowsers prefer to use the term "dowsing," instead of "divining," for this ancient method of discovering hidden substances under the earth. Hazel rods, cut in a fork shape, are the traditional tools for dowsing, though rowan wood and willow were also used; ash, too, had its place, and now metal rods, silk threads, and even nylon are used. Many farmers I have seen dowsing in the countryside where I live frown on any ceremony connected with the actual cutting of the hazel rods and simply cut the appropriate shape. So, if you want to try dowsing yourself—for water, treasure, minerals, or even archaeological finds—set about it thus:

Concentrate on what you are looking for, then grasp the two-pointed hazel rod by the ends of the fork with the bottom of the "Y" away from you. Walk gently (reflectively!) around the ground, and if you are properly attuned you will begin to receive transmissions from the object, or the water. Usually the rod begins to vibrate, and the end almost droops toward the source of energy.

This takes some practice; however, it is something that may make you feel closer to the earth's energies, and is worth bearing with until you have some success. If you can, learn at the feet of a master—try asking an experienced dowser to show you how to do it.

THE COLORS OF WISDOM AND FORGIVENESS

Green—the color of nature in full celebration—is associated with wisdom; the specific green, however, is not the emerald or the deep foresty green of the later reed moon (the chapter covering HOME AND HEARTH—pages 184-195); it is, instead, the olive green that comes from many ivies and trees of the autumn period. This color has the effect of slowing us down a little, and perhaps even inviting us to be grateful for the more subdued greens of the waning year. Mulberry is also in the spectrum of colors of wisdom, because it represents strength and vibrancy, but without aggressive energy. This was an expensive dye to extract in the Middle Ages, but was long lasting and much valued. In England, the Royal House of York used "murray" (a contraction of "mulberry") and blue as its colors.

A blending of the two represents reflection, calm, pensiveness, and mental activity and thought. They are my first choice for all of my files and stationery concerned with my study, and I burn candles in olive and mulberry when I am preparing for my exams to help me think through the work with clarity and to encourage my brain to work well!

If you want your brain ticking over well—but meditatively, perhaps, rather than creatively—buy yourself a present of a coffee mug in these hues, or tie ribbons around an existing favorite, and "breathe in" the colors. Let your thoughts run free, and allow your mind to achieve a particular level of concentration; play some gentle music to engage your mind still further. All this preparation is warranted before tackling important scholastic work, or revising for a test.

THE SCENTS OF WISDOM

Certain scents "switch on" the mind, enabling it to focus more easily and aiding our mental alertness. The acquisition of knowledge—and wisdom—is largely about making the best use of our very considerable mental capabilities. If we think of our brain as the most elaborate computer ever created and realize how lost we are with a brand new PC that is more sophisticated than one we've been used to unless we have time and clear instructions on how to use it, then we may be able to grasp just how little we really know about the potential of our minds.

If we can focus clearly on any task—that is, direct all our energy and attention to the issue at hand—we will achieve greater results for our efforts. Those who focus properly come at the top of their class, whatever that "class" is. They remember things better, and they understand the myriad ramifications of and interconnections between related areas. There are clearly some scents that push our brains into greater mental alertness, and harnessing these is a great aid to acquiring wisdom and knowledge.

Just to get your mind engaged in daily tasks that require concentration (especially study), inhale a few drops of rosemary and lemon essential oils on a tissue or in a burner. Using a scented tissue is an easy way to renew concentration and clarity if you are taking an exam or going for an interview at which you must show mental dexterity and a familiarity with many points.

If you are preparing for an exam, presentation, or lecture, try adding lemon, rosemary, and lavender oils to your bath, and really clearing your mind as you breathe in the steamy concoction. If you have to prepare for something completely new, select a blend of oils that make a rather unusual choice, so that you don't cloud your mind with memories connected

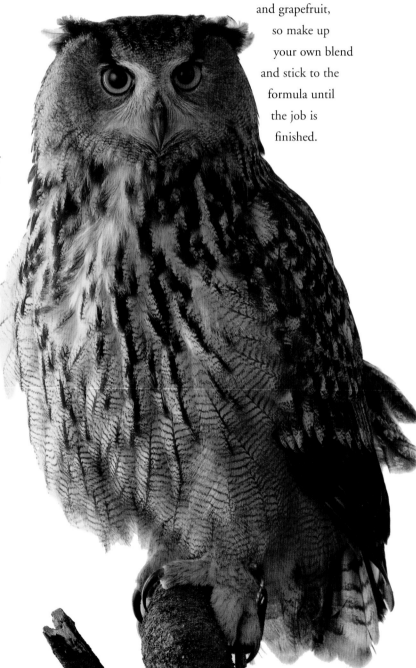

with other things as well. Scent definitely triggers memories—and you want to use this to your advantage, not to cause an overload! Other oils you can choose that stimulate the mind and help you to focus and think clearly are basil, bergamot, ginger, and grapefruit, so make up your own blend and stick to the formula until the job is finished.

THE SYMBOLS OF WISDOM. Remember that knowledge alone is not wisdom: wisdom is the ability to turn knowledge into sound behavior, to be guided toward a beneficial outcome for you and those around you. Even in a love relationship, one may have knowledge of certain truths about the loved one, but it will require wisdom to know how to deal with these facts to ensure the smooth flow of the relationship. WISDOM IS BEYOND KNOWLEDGE.

Meditating on, and incorporating into your life, any of the following symbols should serve as a reminder to think through the ultimate ramifications of all you do. In magic, awareness is the key: to be aware that every action has a connected reaction is an important truth. Always think ahead to what the repercussions may be, instead of acting hastily.

OWLS, BOOKS, SCROLLS, STYLUS, AND PAPER are all symbolic of learning, and magic ritual to encourage daily use of your wisest faculties should draw on some of these emblems. If you are preparing important work, or studying, or beginning a new college life, burn a candle on the eve of your new adventure, and find one of these symbols (even in a picture) to rest beside your name, underneath the candle. The candle should be olive green or mulberry in color and could be scented with one of the oils listed opposite. You should ask for a blessing on your venture: ask that your senses remain strongly with you, and that wise behavior attend your actions and inform your moves.

A **HAZEL STAFF** (or divining rod) has already been mentioned on page 137: dowse for relaxation and focused thought before an important mental challenge. Equally, adding hazelnuts and hazelnut oils to your diet will act as brain food, and as a reminder that you should act with serene wisdom in your daily endeavors. Incorporate the symbols (or strew the nuts) around your work space for their magical properties.

The most potent magical symbol for luck in gaining knowledge and achieving wisdom is the **MULBERRY TREE**. I use a mulberry leaf, twig, or berry in any magic required for wise meditation. Even before deciding what course of action to take, I burn a candle and meditate on a mulberry leaf to ask for guidance. As a child, I was fonder of the fragrant mulberry tree than of any other in the garden. Mulberries are still the taste of my happy childhood, reminding me to be happy in the simplest of things.

TAROT IX, the Wise Hermit, is a powerful symbol in the magic of learning. Make yourself a talisman for an auspicious start to a new education, or job concerned with education, using this card. You might make yourself a cushion for your study chair or work seat, comprising your own name, a benediction for learning, and the symbol of **TAROT ARCANUM IX**. As you make it, think of being a proponent of the wisdom of the centuries: think of being unhurried in decision, and just in arriving at a course of action. Stuff the pillow with herbs related to mental agility: rosemary, of course, and lavender, basil, thyme, even lemon peel.

A **BOTTLE OF WITCH HAZEL, AN HOURGLASS** (wisdom is concerned very much with patience), **A SNAKE, SERPENT, OR DRAGON, AND A SNAIL** (again for patience) are all concerned with acquiring wisdom. An olive branch, or tree, will remind you of the constant need for forgiveness. A wise soul knows how important all these attributes are and how far to temper one's actions with kindness and understanding. This, of course, does not always mean giving in to another's plans or wishes. When you need to be strong, to stand by a decision you have made that you know is wise, even in the face of pressure (emotional blackmail, perhaps), surround yourself with any of these emblems of great power, burn a candle, inhale the scents of the mind, and stick serenely to your cause.

All the magic of wisdom draws on the elements of heightened senses: the ear to the ground, listening for the secrets of the earth; the nose in the wind, detecting scent and movement; the sight applied to clouds, earth, and trees, for signs of change; the tongue still—so that you listen, instead of talking. Draw on these images as part of your everyday magic making to learn to be adept. Remember that speech is silver, but silence is golden.

MASTER SPELL 1: **TO AID IN ABSORBING KNOWLEDGE.** This master spell is designed to intensify your mental powers and prepare you to take on any knowledge with serenity and confidence. With minor adaptations, it will work just as well for someone taking their driving test as for someone facing exams.

YOU WILL NEED

An hourglass; 1 large off-white church candle infused with rosemary oil; some music you enjoy relaxing to; about 1 yard of olive green or mulberry ribbon; beautiful paper on which to write a personal pledge; an olive-green velvet pouch; 9 hazelnuts.

MOON PHASE: *Any, but especially full*

Begin the spell by turning up your hourglass and watching the sands drift through it for a moment. The whole spell should unfold over the duration of the hourglass's emptying. Pledge to be patient in life—to allow good things in you to distill properly.

Light your candle, and put on some soft, classical, or instrumental music that helps you to feel relaxed and peaceful, but at the same time thoughtful. Bind the ribbon around your brow, and imagine your brain feeling receptive, flexible, and hungry for knowledge. Imagine the candlelight and the ribbon penetrating the dark corners of your mind, illuminating it with knowledge and information, and imagine your brain becoming more alive. See if you can picture more of your brain actually being engaged. Vividly see a further sector of your mind waking up, ready to take on new facts and discover more capacity. Close your eyes and concentrate on what lies ahead: if you are studying, pause to consider the material you need to be familiar with; if you are about to take a test, sweep gently over the subject in a kind of video montage that recalls highlights of it.

Open your eyes and look at the candle. Be determined: see yourself successful in the hours from now right through to completion of your important task.

Write on the paper a pledge to be more receptive to new facts and aware of broader issues—to listen and learn more. In your own words, pledge not to be "closed" to any information or subject; promise to spend time actively gleaning more from life—of people's characters, makeup, and psychological disposition, as well as of history, literature, technology, or whatever else fascinates you. Sign the paper and date it; finish with a postscript asking for success in the venture ahead, or whatever situation has inclined you to cast this spell (you could write simply, "exam luck" or something similar). Put the paper in the velvet pouch with the hazelnuts. Do not hurry these actions.

Inhale the light, the scent, the music, and think again about the subject that has prompted your magic; if it is a test or exam, or the presentation of a lecture, speech, or other material, think—while looking at the candle flame and smelling the rosemary—about the information you are required to retain. Say some of the key things out loud.

Let the candle burn down for the remainder of the hour. Finally, unbind the ribbon from your brow and tie the pouch closed with it. Take it with you to your exam, or whatever the occasion may be.

MASTER SPELL 11: **TO HEIGHTEN YOUR SENSES.** This spell is not about acquiring knowledge, but about preparing your senses to perform at their peak—whether for learning, thinking, socializing, or any other situation where peak performance is required.

YOU WILL NEED

A talisman made of silver or gold: choose a deer, a hare, or a rabbit, or, if you prefer, a dog, cat, or horse; a handful of herbs and fresh flowers for crushing to release their fragrance; a short length of mulberry-colored ribbon.

MOON PHASE: *Any*

Choose a bright early morning, preferably when the sun is just rising and the moon is still up. If you are a city dweller, go to a park or a stretch of clear, green land; if you live in the country, make the most of a tranquil setting. Hold up your talisman—first to the moon before she sets, and then to the sun as he rises. This could be a silver or gold brooch, a charm of one of the animals above, or possibly a little ceramic or glass figure if this is all you can find. The animals listed symbolize the most alert and still qualities in the animal kingdom; the hare, in particular, is a special favorite for this because it is the messenger of the moon and thought to be one of the shapes assumed by a witch if she has to disappear because of danger.

Ask for the secrets of day and night; ask for a oneness with the creation; ask for special powers to see without always being seen, to hear without always being heard, to smell without being smelled.

Now sit and gently crush some of the herbs and flowers, one at a time, in your hand, releasing their aroma. Good choices

are early violets, primroses, jonquils, dianthus, and any of the herbs available at the time. The most appropriate is one that is quite subtly scented. Encourage your senses to open completely and take on the feel, look, and fragrance of every individual plant. Make sure you could recognize it again with your eyes blindfolded! Know it by feel as well as by smell. Do this with each herb/flower.

Now put your ear to the earth, and listen. Close your eyes, and listen to the sounds of the earth stirring: birds, distant traffic, crunching twigs, and moving branches. Listen until sounds you never normally bother to pick out emerge with such clarity that you can almost hear the electricity wires humming, or someone's kettle singing! You might hear your own breath, your heart, even your watch ticking.

Look at everything with new eyes: take in the exact color of the sky; the trees in early light; the ground moist with dew; the precise hue of your sweater, or even your skin, in the morning light. Now offer up your animal talisman again to the moon and sun, and quietly walk home, trying hard not to be heard, but listening to everything, looking at everything, smelling all the scents on the way back. Remember the exquisite sensations, and vow to carry these with you more often—to train your senses to brim with awareness and feeling.

Carry your talisman, tied with the ribbon, whenever you need your senses to be most alive.

CELEBRATION

VINE MOON

This chapter examines the vine moon—the last summery moon, as it arrives at the autumn equinox, a moment of unabashed joy and celebration. Recipes for feasting will show how we can slip "magic" ingredients into everyday food to achieve a powerful, enchanting hold on life and buoy up the spirits of everyone around us—but as ever, we must do this with integrity. Recipes are given for flower- and herb-flavored dishes, and for feast wines, which were always at the heart of the celebrations associated with the time of the vine moon—the nicest of these is the champagne cocktail, which has a lemony flavor and strongly aphrodisiac effect. This moon also governs "binding spells," which use the vine to bind any situation, from marriage to a relationship that is threatening to break up. Covering the month of September, this moon and moment are ideal to let your hair down and appreciate the natural rhythms of the earth's cycles, our part in working with them, and the bounty this happiest of marriages yields to us.

The Autumn Equinox. Check the exact date yearly—it will be close to September 21st in the northern hemisphere, March 21st in the south. Daylight and night are once again balanced perfectly, opening our perceptions both to the daylight/obvious and the nighttime/arcane. Our intuition and logic are in equal measure now, so this is a time for action rather than thought. The earth's energy is changing, and we must respond to it.

Fruits and grains are used in ritual; a traditional libation of cider or ale is often poured around the trees to bless their spirits and ensure their strength in the winter months. Pinecones, acorns, and gourds are treated and varnished and placed around the house to ensure prosperity and repeated harvest, and to give thanks for present abundance.

While day and night are equal, it is a ritual time, as at the Spring Equinox, for affairs concerning balance and harmony. This is the moment, then, to patch up quarrels, heal rifts, and work on personal growth that springs from a balanced frame of mind.

Rituals for Peace and Harmony

Early in the morning, make up your own ritual, centering it around symbols of peace and balance—scales, the symbols of Libra, or Yin and Yang, the olive branch, or anything else you like. This is a good time to make a talisman for peace and the ending of arguments by creating simple muslin sachets or little pillows from the herbs in your own garden—however small. Embroider together your own initials with those of people you care for and wish to see balanced with your energies. Fill the pouches or pillows with late September herbs such as lavender,

rose petals, vervain, rosemary, and mint. Keep one, and give another as a gift to your friend.

To heal a serious rift, plant a little tree (even in a pot), putting paper slips with the names of you and your discordant friend under the tiny roots, then tend the tree to grow accord between you again. As at all solar festivals, end the day with some kind of social feast, with candles or a barbecue to honor the sun's changing mood!

VINE MOON—MOON OF CELEBRATION AND HARVEST. Colors: SILVER, BURGUNDY. Scents: EUCALYPTUS, BENZOIN, MANDARIN. Number: 10.

The vine is the active symbol of work well rewarded. As such, it might be an emblem of what we hope for in life: the combination of a wise marriage with nature, diligence regarding our duty, a little luck from above, and a well-earned culmination in festivity following work completed.

"And still she slept an azure-lidded sleep,
In blanched linen, smooth, and lavender'd,
While he from forth the closet brought a heap
Of candied apple, quince, and plum, and gourd;
With jellies smoother than the creamy curd,
And lucent syrops, tinct with cinnamon;
Manna and dates, in argosy transferr'd
From Fez; and spiced dainties, every one,
From silken Samarcand to cedar'd Lebanon."
"THE EVE OF ST. AGNES"
JOHN KEATS

In magic, the vine is a potent symbol. The passion vine is religious, exotic, resilient. Blueberry and blackberry vines stand for protection and resilience; grapevines further suggest prosperity and a dream link with the past. Hops are connected with healing. All the vines can be used in magic spells for binding—as in a contract, an agreement between people, a love relationship that is becoming more serious or indeed threatening to break away—and to bless children or other loved ones as they must go away from you.

The main purpose of the vine moon in the magical calendar, however, concerns justified feasting and joyous thanksgiving. This, then, is largely a cooking chapter, and it will also demonstrate ways of showing a festive spirit in everyday life—or how to make magic in any celebratory situation. It reminds us of the need for enthusing in life—of spreading warmth and happiness, of helping ourselves and others to balance duty and pressure with outright merriment.

The symbols of the magic celebration are mostly foods associated with harvest, for in this period of the year there are variations on harvest festivals from late September through October (embracing Hallowe'en), right up to Thanksgiving in November.

The colors are also associated with the ripening vines. In the early moist, even frosty, mornings, heavy dew brings a silvery sheen to the vines, and the deep burgundy color of the grapes is sometimes matched by the dark reddish hue of the leaves touched by light frost. These, then, are the colors of ripeness: they have a surreal effect on the senses, and used magically, they inject *joie de vivre* into our being.

Here, we will perform the ceremony of cakes and ale—almost an altar to feasting. We will brew an ale, but also make a champagne cocktail—a townies' wine, in case you think the cider ale sounds a bit countrified. We will also make gardenia, lavender, and rose ice creams and send all our friends ribbon-tied cards to celebrate life.

SPREADING EUPHORIA

Now we send magic everywhere by hanging bunches of ribbons, flowers, and pendulous ornaments; this is the moment of "festooning." All the colors used up to date should be tied, rainbow style, around the life you lead in September.

Oils for burning are eucalyptus, melissa, lavender, benzoin, and mandarin. Send your friends cards written with perfumed ink (adding three or four drops of sandalwood, rose attar, neroli, or bergamot to the ink pot and shaking well: all these oils are for joy), tied around the middle with a rainbow of colored ribbons and spattered with a drop or two of one of these oils. Send a prayer for their good fortune and happiness before you seal the envelope—which you could also cram with a few heavily scented rose petals.

Bake simple cakes covered with thick whipped cream and then strewn with late rose petals. Take them to friends who have been feeling a bit down; ask them to "make a wish" (an old Pagan cakes-and-ale prayer if ever there was one) as they cut the cake and to believe in its power to bring the wish home. Invite other friends to afternoon teas and serve the meal with whipped cream and rose petals. Beautiful late sunsets will make a perfect backdrop to wishing magic shared in celebratory teas with friends. Offer unusual teas made from gardenia or borage flowers, or jasmine if you still have some blooming; all three lift the spirits and are beloved of the gods.

Wine in beautiful glassware to share with many friends is another beautiful vine moon custom: the glasses must be the best you can afford, glinting in the late sun/early moon. Use the champagne cocktail, or a good sparkling wine.

CELEBRATION MAGIC IN EVERYDAY LIFE

- Give small nosegays of flowers to people who look sad or stressed.

- Pot up autumn seeds for friends, with "wishes" (written on tiny bits of paper) "sown" into the soil.

- Fill your car with a rainbow of balloons, and take a friend driving into the country to watch a late sunset.

- Make a floral wreath on your door as though it were Christmas, weaving colored ribbons, grapes, and late flowers into it. Wish for joy as you work, then ask friends around for dinner.

- Wear colorful clothes deliberately to spread color from your footsteps everywhere you go.

MAGIC IN FOOD. The idea of food magic is that certain substances inherent in herbs and flowers, when combined in particular ways, alter our perception or state of being for a while. Now that we have been able to test the properties of herbs more effectively, we can understand the claim better than before; for it is certainly true that the complex chemicals in herbs, which are natural rather than synthesized, have a direct impact on our health and well-being. The age-old tradition, then, is to incorporate these "magical ingredients" into our menu.

WITCHES' BREAD

I have no idea whether this recipe is known to other Wiccans, but my grandmother used to make it and always called it "witches' bread." Perhaps it was partly self-mocking. However, from what I can tell, it is very close to the recipe for soda bread—with a few herbs added for magic and flavor. It is very easy to make and does not require any yeast.

The herbs used vary, but a combination of marjoram and rosemary was always at the center of it: the former seems to have a tonic effect and can also help to counteract irritability, while the latter, being antiseptic, helps to preserve foods but also stimulates the brain and seems to have a beneficial effect on our cholesterol count. The other herb my grandmother used was calendula (marigold), or if available, wild chrysanthemum. The first is known as an antidepressant, and the second was believed to bestow long life. Indeed, it now seems it may have anti-cancer properties. Consume this bread, then, for a long and healthy life, active mind, and the ability to cope with stress. It should be broken apart, not cut.

When eaten with friends, the bread will form the center of a simple but delicious feast with both physical and spiritual properties.

YOU WILL NEED

2 cups of white flour; 2 cups of wholewheat flour; a pinch of salt; 2 teaspoons of baking soda; 2 teaspoons of baking powder; 3¹/₂ tablespoons of butter (lard was traditional); 3 tablespoons of oatmeal; fresh herbs (as opposite); a small beaten egg; 17 fl. oz. of buttermilk (or milk soured with vinegar and lemon juice).

Sift together the flours, salt, baking soda, and baking powder, then cut or rub in the butter and oatmeal so that the mixture resembles fine breadcrumbs. Toss the finely cut herbs through the mixture. Make a well in the center of the bowl, and add the beaten egg and buttermilk, using a knife to combine the ingredients. Knead very lightly against the sides of the bowl, then shape into two rounds—like cakes. Put them into well-greased 8 inch round pans, and cut a cross into the top of the bread right across the diameter, so that you effectively mark out four quarters. Dust the top lightly with flour, or brush with a little milk. Bake for about 30–35 mins at 400°F. Turn out onto a wire rack to cool.

THE ICE CREAMS

Ice cream was formerly a luxury at the end of a meal. The old method of making it required access to an ice house, an elaborate wooden bucket with a spindle for churning, and the use of salt to boost the cooling effect of the ice. All in all, it was a special achievement to make ice cream—which we have forgotten, because of the ease of doing so now with modern ice-cream makers.

The addition of exotic flowers—lavender, gardenia, and rose—intensified the exotic quality of the ice cream itself; but besides providing flavor and fragrance, the flowers have potent magical properties which affect the one who consumes it deliciously.

- LAVENDER eases away aches, headache, nausea, and tiredness—which makes it a restorative for the end of a meal or long feast (or even a long day at the office). It is also widely regarded as an aphrodisiac— perhaps simply because of the qualities already mentioned and the fact that it counters bad breath.

- ROSE reputedly also has great powers to counter unpleasant breath; it has a long history of use medicinally as well as in culinary and cosmetic preparations. The scent cheers the senses and may have a calming effect on the heart, while the petals—made into a tea and used in cooking—are an excellent tonic for those who are convalescing or run down. The petals are also traditionally used in the treatment of stress and anxiety—which may account for their use in magical cookery.

- GARDENIA is the most exotic of the three, and is the most magical in the imagination of the witch working love recipes. Perhaps it is the intensely sweet fragrance; and even today,

in Chinese medicine, the flowers and fruits are acknowledged to lift the spirits and be inspirational.

A TRIO OF ICE CREAMS

These ice creams are especially easy to prepare. They are all made without the aid of an ice-cream maker, relying instead on alcohol to raise the temperature at which the mixture freezes and prevent ice crystals from forming. There is no need to whip the mixture at intervals.

YOU WILL NEED

2 large gardenia flowers; 3 or 4 fragrant roses—gallica or damask types are best; several sprigs of lavender flowers (preferably fresh, or dried if necessary); 3 x 1/3 cup of superfine sugar; 3 x 6 large eggs, separated; 3 x 1 1/4 pt. of heavy cream; 3 x 1 fl. oz. of cognac or kirsch.

For each ice cream, infuse the flowers individually in an airtight jar with the sugar for three or four days, shaking gently each day. Over these few days the flavors will develop in each jar of sugar.

Make each mixture separately. For each of the three ice creams, grease a large charlotte or gelatin mold thoroughly. Set the flowers aside and beat the individual sets of egg yolks with each of the sugars until each mixture is pale and fluffy. Now whip the cream and incorporate the flowers as you beat it until thick. (For the gardenia, it is best to tear the flower petals to release the remaining fragrance before adding them to the cream.) Fold each of the creams into each of the egg mixtures.

Now beat each set of whites in a chilled bowl until very stiff peaks form. Fold the whites gently into the other mixtures with a metal spoon, and add the alcohol now. You can add extra petals from the individual flowers if you want more texture in the ice creams—but don't overdo it. Add a few drops of lemon juice to deepen the lavender color of the lavender ice cream; a few drops of glycerine added to the rose will deepen its color a little, too.

Pour each individual mixture into one of the molds, and cover with plastic wrap. Freeze for at least 6 hours, or overnight, to let the flavors intensify. Unmold by immersing the mold in very hot water for a few seconds, and turn each ice cream onto a serving plate. They can be decorated casually with fresh flowers and—for the gardenia—leaves, and served immediately.

These ice creams make a literally magical end to any ordinary dinner: save them for someone you really love, to create a mood of ease and abundant good humor.

CAKES AND ALE

The center of any harvest festival is bread, and the idea that consuming food made the matter it consisted of live again—and that the symbolic connection between the food and a corporal idea was borne aloft by eating it, as in the Christian ceremony of Holy Communion—is behind the ritual of cakes and ale.

Cakes and ale form the apogee of a celebratory feast: this is the completion of the cycle of spirit and transcendent being. The cake is representative of the material world; the ale is the spirit of fire and air, as well as water. Both are usually dedicated to the deities; and again, the rite of eating the food signifies taking on divine strength and grace within the individual or the company.

Always bless your bread, and ask that it return manifold. For this reason, the rite of cakes and ale is largely concerned with health, prosperity, and fertility.

SIMPLE CELEBRATION CAKE

This recipe is fairly typical of several Cornish, and indeed Breton, special afternoon cakes. It is a simple cake but very moist, and tastes delicious straight from the oven: but the secret ingredient is the rose geranium—sometimes, apple geranium is substituted.

The effect of this herb is to flavor the cake subtly and make something delicate and ethereal out of it, while at the same time the antidepressant properties of the herb seem literally to lift our spirits and make us more inclined to put our cares away and feel positive.

YOU WILL NEED

1 1/2 cups of flour; 1/4 teaspoon of baking powder; 3 large eggs; 3/4 cup of melted butter; 3/4 cup of white sugar; 2 tablespoons of kirsch or brandy; 4 or 5 rose geranium leaves, torn apart loosely (if you use cider brandy, use apple geranium leaves instead); extra geranium leaves or flowers to garnish.

Sift the flour and baking powder into a bowl, and mix in the eggs with a wooden spoon, then add the butter, sugar, and kirsch or brandy. Once the mixture has a smooth consistency, add the geranium leaves. The mixture should be relatively liquid.

Butter a medium-sized cake pan and line it with waxed paper or baking parchment. Pour the mixture into the pan and bake at 400°F for 25–30 minutes. Let the cake cool, then turn out and decorate with geranium leaves or flowers.

Consume the cake while it is still warm—"blood temperature"—and dedicate a slice of it to the gods. Afterward, crumble that slice for the birds, or over the soil. The cake has a definite impact on the senses and will lift your spirits even if you have had a stressful day. Thus, if you partake of it with a lover, you will feel more sanguine and lively together.

CHAMPAGNE COCKTAIL—A LOVE POTION

The most celebratory drink I know of is a guaranteed magic draft. Borage is one of the witch's most magic plants, for it cheers the senses utterly. This seems to be because it stimulates the production of epinephrine, or adrenaline, and it has a long association as the herb of euphoria. Put into ice cubes, it makes a wonderful garnish for any summer drink. It has the magic power in champagne to intoxicate the senses and entice another being to think wonderfully of you—use wisely. First make a syrup . . .

YOU WILL NEED

2 or 3 borage leaves, and the same number of flowers; 2 tablespoons of sugar or honey; 1/2 cup of water; juice of 1 lemon; a sugar cube; one or two drops of Angostura bitters; a small shot of good brandy; champagne; 1–2 extra borage flowers to garnish.

Bring the first four ingredients gently to the boil while dissolving the sugar in the liquid, and reduce until a thick syrup is produced. Chill thoroughly.

Saturate a sugar cube with the syrup in the bottom of each flute glass, add the bitters and the brandy, then top with good champagne. Add one or two more flowers for garnish. Share with your lover and leave all your cares behind . . . . BLISS!

THE ALE

A traditional English West Country ale for special occasions is effectively an apple cider punch—which uses plenty of hedgerow produce to give it an extra kick. The key is to infuse the gin with the sloes and subsequently absorb all the tonic properties of this beautiful blue-black fruit from the blackthorn tree. The wonderful pinkish color it creates with the gin is guaranteed to lift the spirits anyway—but do not drive afterward. The longer you let the sloe gin mature, the more delicious and potent the properties of the drink—a year is not too long. To half a bottle of gin add ³/₈ cup of sugar, 3¹/₂ cups of sloes, 1 cup of whole almonds, and a teaspoon of brandy for flavor. Macerate the almonds, or bruise them, slit the sloes open with a sharp knife, and bottle the nuts and fruit with the brandy, sugar, and gin. Seal the bottle, and shake well each day for at least two weeks. Store it away from the light for at least a month.

Then, to make the ale….

YOU WILL NEED

2 quarts of hard cider; sloe gin (as above); 1 cup of sherry (or rum); 2 lemons; 2 oranges; 3 tablespoons of sugar; plenty of fresh lemon balm and mint leaves; chilled mineral water.

Carefully combine the three alcoholic beverages in a large punch bowl; slice the citrus fruits, peels intact, and add to the mixture with the sugar. Crush the lemon balm and mint, add to the bowl, chill, and dilute with sparkling mineral water to serve. Wow!

The ale and either the bread or cake can now be used to toast the spirit of prosperity and long life, as well as offering to the deity. The server should pass the bread and drink to the left (in other words, clockwise), as it is bad luck to go "widdershins" (or counterclockwise) for a celebratory rite. Always return some of the cakes and ale to the earth at the conclusion of the feasting.

Remember to serve your drink in vessels tied with burgundy or silver ribbon (or both), and to make a wish for general prosperity and health as you do so.

Remember, too, to give thanks for all the blessings you receive in your life.

MASTER SPELL: **TO ENSURE THE SUCCESS OF A PARTY OR SPECIAL EVENT.**

This spell is designed for all guests to share in at a special occasion: it will suit any, so there are few variations. The vines are present to "bind" the joy to the spell participants, and are appropriate whether you are celebrating a wedding, naming day or christening, graduation, birthday, anniversary, housewarming, new job—in fact absolutely anything. The goal, of course, is to continue the joy from this day on, ad infinitum. . . .

YOU WILL NEED

Vines; 1 yard each of silver and burgundy ribbon; a clean white (or cream) pillar candle; name(s) of the person or people whom the celebration honors, written on a small piece of paper with perfumed ink; several needles; silver and burgundy balloons (any quantity), into which silver stars have been inserted.

MOON PHASE: *Any, but waxing would be good*

Decorate the venue with some vines: include passionflower vine, if you can get it, otherwise grape and ivy are lovely.

Before the main festivities are under way, tape out the ribbon into a pentagram star (five points). Use both colors, and lay one over the other. Place the candle in the middle, with the name(s) of the person or people concerned on paper underneath the candle. Ask the participants to join in the wish.

The spell will now be "formed" when all the guests join in the toast and, taking a needle warmed at the candle in the stars, burst the balloons so that the stars descend on the speller or couple or—numbers permitting—all the guests as well. The principal person or people honored should take home a piece of the vine, twined around the left arm, to bind the joy of this occasion to them prosperously, now and in the future.

VARIATIONS ON THE MASTER SPELL

IF THE CELEBRATION IS FOR A WEDDING,

put some confetti and some orange blossom fragrance into the balloons, along with the stars. When they burst, the room will have a magical orange scent—which is lucky for weddings.

IF THE OCCASION IS A CHRISTENING OR NAME DAY,

choose rose petals and fragrance for a girl, dried herbs and citrus notes for a boy, and do the same as for the variation above.

FALL

Fall

has started, preparing us for the change in our psyche as we head toward winter. The days are shorter and colder, the colors of the leaves alter, and fruits are ripening, but we feel invigorated. For many people, fall is the most vivid and wonderful of the seasons, bearing comparison to a growing personal maturity and a delight in the ripeness of life. Now is the time for completing outdoor tasks and drawing inspiration from nature's myriad activities. We, too, can plant seeds that will live on through the colder months and germinate as projects the following spring. Make an effort to acknowledge the harvest this year—either at Hallowe'en or at Thanksgiving. Note the changes, celebrate them, and respond to them. Our senses and energy are heightened by the blend of sunshine and crisp, cool weather. Enjoy it! Element: water. Direction: west.

THE MAGICAL SPIRAL OF STRENGTH. The season is spiraling toward its wintry rest. Life is ebbing, and this can be a very happy experience, turning inward to hear your own needs. The spiral is a very positive symbol, ancient in Celtic magic, sacred to the idea of descent into periods of test and trial, with a safe return. Like Ariadne in the labyrinth, in the ancient Greek legend, holding on to the thread means we know we can come back again.

One of your seasonal tasks is to embroider or make a spiral. This may be contrived from threads or ribbons, in the garden with stones, or you may choose to weave a basket to emblematize the move through new knowledge and tests of your strength. If you have no confidence in your powers with the needle or in weaving, try simply drawing an elaborate spiral, possibly writing your own words of spells and incantation in between the lines. In the making of it, you will gain a powerful tool that will enable you to rise above adversity. No matter how others test you, you will still know where you are bound. The spiral reminds us that most demands in life are tests of the strength of our minds—our recovery of optimism, of will, or our capacity to find a way around obstacles with cheerful determination.

Your garden spiral could be laid with stones leading to a central feature—a potted plant, a water-filled vessel, or even a symbol of reorientation such as an armillary sphere, a sundial, or a compass point. Plant the spiral with little crocuses, snowdrops, or other early bulbs, to give you strength and powers of recovery as well as luck with the first signs of spring.

If you embroider a spiral, choose magical colors: pink for love, red for passion, green for health, purple and indigo for spirituality, blue for protection. Weave in tiny symbols—hearts, flowers, shells, keys, coins, or a house. According to your choice, you will be able to overcome tests in any of these areas. The spiral is your lucky compass, ever pointing you toward home.

SPARKLING SPIRALS

Fall is the perfect moment for celebrations with fireworks. All the fire festivals were held at this time. Make a cake and place sparklers—representing the spark of energy—on top, rather than candles. Or set out a tiny altar in the garden using outdoor candles, wind chimes, and spirals, for these are the symbols of autumn. The spiral shows the earth's energy coiling itself for retraction and then re-launching. Autumn, like spring, is a season of balance between light and dark, warm and cool—your garden altar could reflect the balance shown by the scales in the sign of Libra. Wind chimes recall the power of the westerly winds of autumn, so even if you have only a tiny space in the city to live, hang wind chimes in the window to usher in melodically the magic and power of the west wind.

The element of autumn is water. Place some pebbles in a dish with some sand and water, or grow something hydroponically. Add a sparkler, and honor the fire ceremonies. Make a wish as you light it and envisage your goal achieved.

GROWING SPELLS. Bulbs are strongly magical. The numerous layers enfolded in their skins seem to represent humanity; thus they have a long history of use in spells. Fall is the time to begin a ritual with bulbs, partly because they should be planted now to overwinter and bloom in spring, but also because of the symbolism of something new generated from something old. During the winter months ahead, while the bulb sleeps and prepares to unleash its life in the spring, it is close to the secrets of the unknown, taking its strength from the dark realms. This will imbue the speller with extra powers of hidden wisdom.

YOU WILL NEED
A medium size pot; 1 or more bulbs (tulips, hyacinths, daffodils, amaryllis lilies, or even little snowdrops, crocuses, or grape hyacinths); bulb fiber; a tiny sheet of paper; 1 emblem of love or success (such as a coin, heart-shaped brooch, or other charm).

Choose a really pretty pot to complement your choice of bulb(s). Make your color choice of flower count; yellow would be well suited to money spells, whereas pinks or reds suit love. If you wish to start over again in love, because of breaks or bad luck in the recent past, choose a white flower. If you want a more exciting life/career, etc., choose an appropriately exotic bulb. Choose something scented, like a hyacinth, if you want to transmit thought to someone a long way away.

Write a little note or spell in your own words, keeping them simple, then place your scrap of paper and the charm deep in the soil in the pot. Plant your bulb(s) above and tuck the remaining soil around. As you water the bulb after planting, say: gently "*May I, too, nurture my inner self, and emerge like a butterfly in spring.*"

Cover the pot with dark plastic, and place it somewhere cool. Remove the plastic after about six weeks, near to midwinter, then speak loving words to it every day for several weeks until the green shoots look strong. Your area of interest will be gradually sprouting too, and, as the bulb flowers, you will see your life blossom anew.

HERBAL THERAPY. Try never to miss the magic of a moment. At this time of the year, as the sap of trees and flowers returns to their root systems, we too are preparing to turn inward. Use these last magnificent days to prolong the joy of the fall harvest.

GIFTS AND AMULETS

Gather in your late summer herbs, and make herb pillows and amulets from the bounty of garden and hedges. Amulets are small pouches stuffed with different herbs chosen for love or success, into which some of your own magic words have been spoken. Cut lavender and rose for love pillows, mint to rid yourself of negativity, marjoram and rosemary for protection, lemon balm and basil for success in business. Make simple pillows or bags, and give some as gifts. If you haven't enough of your own grown herbs, buy one or two pots, and harvest from them.

ONION DIVINATION

A traditional method of divination from the fall garden is to plant an onion with a question written below. If you cannot choose between two or more possible paths, plant onions in the early fall. For each possibility—such as wondering which lover is truer, or which course to take, or which home to move to—put the name of each of your two choices under an onion bulb in a blue pot. Whichever bulb shoots the first true green shoot will be your stronger option, but don't jump to conclusions—observe the shoots for a week or more, to see whether an early winner shows signs of being overtaken by a rival for strength and beauty.

Now is the time to use the last crop of LAVENDER. Harvest any remaining flower stalks, use the flowers and leaves in herb pillows, tie the rest up in bunches, and hang these up to dry in a warm place. Lavender can be kept like this for months, scenting rooms throughout the winter, or made into little sachets for the linen closet and your drawers to introduce magic and love among your personal things. Lavender is also a crucial ingredient in potpourri. Use your autumn lavender with vervain for a potent love potpourri for the bedroom. Before you go to bed, stir it with your left ring finger, and ask your dreams any question concerning love affairs. You will be directed to the answer as you sleep.

BORAGE, a vital ingredient in summer love potions, is a wonderful divination herb in the fall. Its prolific and beautiful blue flowers appear right into the coldest weather, lasting until the frosts. Place one flower on your forehead with your index finger, light a candle of the same blue, and ask a question concerning your fate. You should soon receive the answer. A flower can likewise be pressed into a book of divination, such as an oracle, or a pack of Tarot cards. You will get even clearer insights and should keep the flower there.

ROSE HIPS are the natural follower of the flowers in many fall roses. Collect and make a light tea with them to soothe your spirits when you need to find solutions on a day of headaches. Inhaling rose oil at the same time will make you feel wiser, more forgiving of the world around you, and able to cope with tension.

YARROW stalks also have a long history of use in divination. If you have space to grow this aromatic plant, remove the foliage in the fall, and retain the stalks in a pile. Ask a question requiring a "yes" or "no" answer, close your eyes, and sweep the pile into two roughly equal heaps, then count them. Those to your left say "yes," and those to the right, "no." The greater number in either pile will give the result.

CONJURING THE WIND. Witches have ever been associated with power over the weather. In Britain, where the climate is so changeable, I have confined my own spells to requests for sunny bursts in between bad days, even in summer. I usually manage to get away with a barbecue on a fixed date, or the clouds clearing for an outdoor occasion just long enough to make a good photo or reach the car.

The conjuring of the wind is an old custom, performed in fall when the wind has the job of clearing away the past and preparing for the new. Raising a wind will rid us of depression or apathy, or even purge ill luck. Traditionally, a wind might be conjured up to enhance the chance of escape from trouble. In the tale told me by my grandmother, which bears a close resemblance to some of the features of Keats' "*Ode to Saint Agnes*," it facilitated a young girl's escape from confinement to the arms of her lover, as the house around her, in Volterra, in Italy, actually blew down. It might be best to stop the spell before you achieve a tempest such as that!

A SPELL TO BLOW AWAY ILL FORTUNE. Now the tide in your life may change, and your luck turn for the better in all things.

Go to an open space such as a garden, a park, or by water in the early evening, and look up at the moon. You may use your own words, but your invocation should be somewhat along these lines: "*Gentle Diana, I am presently feeling heavy and oppressed* (you might express the reasons why) *and ask of you a sign of change in my situation. Let me scent the air of change, and send me a breeze, gentle as the zephyr, or a wind, powerful and commanding, to blow away the sadness and restraint that I feel.*" Sprinkle a little salt on the ground and a few drops of water from a little flask or bottle. Look up again at the moon and say: "*Lovely goddess of the bow, lovely lady of the arrows, raise up your hounds, and hunt away my woe.*" You should leave one moon-colored flower, crystal, or gem in the place where you have stood.

During the course of the evening the wind should begin to rise. Do not be surprised, indeed, if a storm may appear that lasts for a day! Make sure you feel at least some of the wind through your hair, and if rain comes, let it wash away your uncertainties.

PROTECTING LOVE. Fall is the appropriate season in which to protect those we want to come home safe. The spell below is applicable whether you have a love going away for a while, or a new love who you want to protect. Put your heart and soul into it.

YOU WILL NEED

A few fresh or dried flowers; a yellow or red-orange autumn leaf; a small flower press frame; colored ink; rose oil.

Begin by choosing your flowers, depending on what you want to say. Autumn flowers available would include Michaelmas daisy (*"I wait for your decision"*), geranium (*"I can wait for you"*), honeysuckle (*"I send you a token of my love"*), hyacinth (blue: *"I dedicate myself to you"*; or white: *"I esteem you greatly"*), cyclamen (*"We will overcome difficulty"*), tiger lily (*"I am passionate about you"*), myrtle (*"I am forever true to you"*), pansy (white for kind thoughts; yellow is *"Oceans part us"*; purple for deep love); rosemary flowers (*"I always remember you"*), guelder rose (*"Autumn love"*), wallflowers (*"Constancy through rain and storm"*). An ash leaf added brings lion-like perseverance; an oak leaf brings courage; holly (*"We will be restored to one another"*);

poplar (*"All will turn out well"*); maple (*"Do not leave me from your thoughts"*); and willow (*"My weeping will end"*). Clover added will bring luck and protection.

Press your flowers and leaves into a pretty ensemble, then write a tiny message between the leaves and petals in beautiful colored ink, which you have scented in the bottle with a few drops of rose oil. If you wish, write out the meanings of the flowers you have chosen. At the bottom, just under the press frame, write your name with that of your loved one and the year in Roman numerals. When the frame is fully ready, hang it someplace where it will catch the light.

Your love will grow stronger in proportion to the strength of your own feelings and your ability to trust your partner.

SAMHAIN: HALLOWE'EN. This festival, the old Celtic New Year, is still the best-known of all, preserving its magical and ritualistic feel thanks mainly to the Celtic presence in America. Hallowe'en concerns magic and rituals of remembering the dead, being—like Imbolc—the moment when the "crack" between the worlds of summer and winter, and life and death, is perceived as being open.

Witches still make Hallowe'en a new year celebration, when memory turns to the loss of loved ones in the past. Divination by all means is favored now, so gather together friends and have oracle parties, look at horoscopes, or practice more traditional forms of divination. Appropriate witches' activities include scrying for the future through smoke or wax dropped in water, in both instances to discern shapes or letters. Nine candles are lit for the memory of friends and relatives departed, and a fire of nine sticks is lit for protection from prying but unwanted spirits. Apples should be woven into ritual, including one apple used in love spells.

If someone you know has lost a relative, you might suggest this practice taken from deep magic. Loving letters were once written and placed in the graves of the great warriors to read when they awoke in the immortal world. The ritual of writing letters to those with whom we have lost contact is both a comfort to the living and a magical thread of the unfinished words that will connect living and dead through the future. Spells for forgiveness and farewell can be written and placed in sacred places—under trees, or into fire, or even at a graveside.

THE LOVE APPLE

One of the loveliest and best-known Hallowe'en rituals concerns divination about love for single women. Brush your hair in front of a mirror while eating an apple (symbol of the goddess of love) to bring a vision of your beloved: if the glow is soft and mellow, the love is true; if the vision engenders fear, the love is fickle. It is particularly poetic—and some say accurate—if you create a mirror by filling a silver dish with water and perform this ceremony on Hallowe'en in the late evening. Often, the lover, apparently coincidentally, comes to visit or calls just after the ceremony!

RESILIENCE

IVY MOON

AUTUMN

IS A TIME TO LOOK AT OUR HEALTH,

VITALITY, AND BEAUTY. RESILIENCE IS THE KEY TO

SURVIVING ALL OF LIFE'S TESTS. IVY IS BELOVED MAGICALLY FOR ITS

TENACITY, ITS RESILIENCE, AND ITS BEAUTY. THE IVY MOON—WHICH

COVERS THE PERIOD FROM THE END OF SEPTEMBER TO LATE OCTOBER—IS ALSO

THE MOON OF BUOYANCY; THIS CONCERNS OUR CAPACITY TO SEE THE BEST IN

EVERYTHING AND KEEP OUR SPIRITS HIGH AT ALL TIMES. THE ESSENCE OF THIS CHAPTER

IS HEALTH, AND ALL MAGIC RELATES EITHER TO REMAINING HEALTHY AND BEAUTIFUL OR

TO RECOVERING HEALTH BEFORE WE ARE IN TRUE CRISIS. THIS INCLUDES MENTAL HEALTH

PROBLEMS, SUCH AS DEPRESSION; AND WE LOOK FOR MAGICAL WAYS TO BOOST OUR

PSYCHOLOGICAL STATE WHEN WE ARE UNDER SIEGE. THE COLORS AND SCENTS FOR

HEALTH ARE LOOKED AT, AND A "MAGIC DIET" IS INCLUDED. A WITCH'S HERB LORE

WAS WHAT TRADITIONALLY DISTINGUISHED HER AS A WITCH. THE MONTH IS

PERHAPS THE MOST FECUND IN NATURE, WHEN THE LAST HEADY DAYS OF

AUTUMN SUNSHINE PROLONG THE BEAUTY OF THE SEASON BEFORE

THE ONSET OF WINTER. IT IS A CELEBRATION OF

HEALTHY MATURITY.

IVY MOON—MOON OF RESILIENCE AND BUOYANCY. Colors: DEEP FOREST-GREEN, BLACK. Scents: ROMAN CHAMOMILE, LAVENDER, GRAPEFRUIT, PEPPERMINT, HYACINTH, MARJORAM, JASMINE, PATCHOULI, ORRIS, SANDALWOOD, ROSEWOOD (the "rainbow of scent"). Number: 11 (the master number).

"Season of mists and mellow fruitfulness.
   Close bosom-friend of the maturing sun:
   Conspiring with him how to load and bless
   With fruit the vines that round the thatch-eaves run."
"To Autumn"
JOHN KEATS

Once ivy is firmly established in any garden it is very difficult to eradicate, and from September into November, in northern climes, it produces wonderful clusters of yellow-green flowers at a time when most other garden plants are dying back. It clings determinedly to old ruined walls and derelict houses; it scrambles over forgotten paths and clothes fallen tree trunks with a new form of life which becomes a haven for other living things.

Since ancient times, the ivy's magical powers have been renowned: as the "enemy of the vine," it has a long association with defeating intoxication, and it is connected with the treatment of headache and migraine. However, it is quite poisonous if strong doses are taken internally, and the expressed juice is now used only as an external compress for aching limbs, swollen feet, and cellulitis, so do not treat yourself with this herb except on professional medical advice.

Ivy is used symbolically in magic, for its tenacity and ability to cling; it is a symbol of good health, as it grows to a ripe age and beautifies during the barren months. The plant stands for optimism; it asks us to believe that good must ultimately prevail, no matter how testing life becomes. When all else is bare, the fingers of green ivy add color and vivacity to naked trees and soil. We should dig deep and breathe in the delicious herbal smell of the life around us. We should cling on. WE SHOULD BE AS RESILIENT AS THE IVY—WHICH SEEMS ABLE TO STAND EVEN THE SEVEREST FROST.

If you have been feeling downhearted or under the weather and tired out, surround yourself with magic images of resilience in the form of rubber and elastic. In everyday magic spells, rubber bands can be used to suggest the capacity to bounce back. Describe a five-pointed star in forest-green ribbon, place your picture in the middle, and put a lovely bouncy rubber ball (tiny and colorful) on top. Pick it up for a few minutes each day and bounce it on the floor, seeing your own face bouncing back into glowing health and rejuvenated action.

THE WITCH'S HERBALL, OR THE DIET OF EVERYDAY MAGICAL HEALTH.
The selection of salad in the supermarket is now so varied that it hardly seems necessary to describe the need for a varied herbal diet to maintain health. However, our ancestors had little access to such a wealth of natural vitamins, and a diet enriched with herbs was often the difference between sickness and health. So, advice on this subject was perhaps the most valuable a witch could give.

The following herbs formed the nucleus of the witch's garden and were prescribed for health and for their magical properties. Undoubtedly, if you vary your diet to include many of them regularly, you will maintain strength and good spirits and rarely be on the sick list, while herbs that help to keep you calm must allay many problems. If you have little space to grow them yourself, many of these herbs are available fresh, either potted or flat-packed, in supermarkets.

SAGE There is an old proverb that runs, *"Why should a man die, who has sage in his garden?"* This herb was the most essential in preserving (and even, it was thought, creating) life. A general tonic for both mind and body, it is highly regarded for its digestive properties—which is why it is a famous accompaniment for fatty meats such as duck, pork, and even lamb—while also being a tonic for the nerves and stimulating to the circulation. This makes it an ideal tea for anyone suffering from stress or exhaustion, and it is wonderful for those who are convalescing. Red (or purple) sage is the correct choice for throat inflammations, but use garden sage plentifully in cooking to keep in good health and promote an efficiently working system. Make a strong decoction of the herb ($^1/_2$ oz. of dried, or 10 fresh, sage leaves steeped in boiling water for ten minutes) to combat skin irritations. This is the most important herb in the witch's medicine cabinet.

CLARY This is another herb that aids digestion, and it adds a delicious flavor to salads and cooked vegetable dishes. Use only a tiny amount. Added to wine or beer, it intensifies the flavor but also has the power to lift the spirits of the imbiber. Definitely worth growing a little—or at least burning the essential oil when you're feeling stretched.

ANGELICA This well-known cake decoration had, in the past, a much more distinguished reputation than we accord it nowadays. Both a stimulant and a tonic herb, grated angelica root was made into a tea ($^1/_2$ oz. of grated root—somewhat like ginger—added to a quart of boiling water, steeped for a quarter of an hour) and consumed if the spirits were low or someone was lethargic. Do not do this too often, or it will prove more stimulating even than coffee.

BORAGE My own favorite for cheering up even the most unpromising day. Make a decoction as a healthy tea (1 oz. in a quart of boiling water, boiled for another minute, then steeped for another ten), or add to chilled wines in summer to stimulate the adrenaline and cause a positive mood swing. Flowers in salads and strewn on iced cakes will contribute to health and well-being—and treat the senses aesthetically, too.

FENNEL The properties of the bulb and seeds are now well noted and are, amongst other things, employed to ease flatulence and indigestion. Italians are hugely (and wisely) fond of the bulb, adding it to salads—and it now appears that it may have especially beneficial results for women, as the chemical properties are somewhat like those of estrogen.

MINTS Don't overdo it, but cooking with mint will naturally freshen your breath, counter mouth complaints, and calm the nerves. An ideal choice of tea to deal with insomnia, mint settles the stomach and also helps to neutralize headache caused by tiredness and nausea. It is very easy to grow in your kitchen window.

TARRAGON The best cure for hiccups I know. Beloved of cooks for its culinary versatility, this herb was originally popular because of its capacity to aid digestion and soothe pain. Tear the leaves and scatter them over chicken and fish dishes at the last minute to keep the properties of the herb in peak form.

CARAWAY A crucial ingredient for flavoring breads, the seeds have properties similar to those of fennel and dill, but are also antispasmodic and thus a good overall health tonic. Add the young shoots of caraway to salads to sweeten the breath and relieve heartburn.

THYME This wonderful little plant is nature's own antibiotic. A cold can be nipped in the bud by making a strong tea from fresh thyme or adding thyme leaves to food. Use the oil, diluted of course, to make a therapeutic rub for the treatment of muscular aches and pains and sciatica, and to bathe in to counter depression. Boiled up with marjoram, thyme lotion (a very strong tea) makes an excellent footbath to cure blisters and corns.

MARJORAM This herb has strong sedative properties, so it must be taken cautiously; however, mild teas certainly aid restfulness. It, too, has good tonic effects and can help to ease menstrual cramps. Apart from soothing inflamed throats and mouth infections, this herb was respected by my grandmother for its ability to relieve hay fever—which she did by saturating absorbent cotton in a strong solution and inhaling it. This can also be an effective treatment for headache. My own discovery concerning this herb is its powerful capacity to heal damaged feet (see thyme, above).

BASIL The plant that needs no one to argue its case as a culinary herb. Medicinally, it has many valued properties—not least that basil tea is very effective in settling bad nerves—

and it is also known to stimulate the brain to work effectively. This makes it an ideal choice for anyone facing exams or other work stress. Wine with basil leaves steeped in it is an effective tonic and—almost certainly—has some aphrodisiac effects. Soups, stews, pasta dishes, vegetable recipes, and salads will all gain immensely from the addition of a few loosely torn basil leaves: *fresh are best.*

WATERCRESS Easily absorbed into soups, sandwiches, and salads, this herb has been used since Roman times in many interesting ways. It was thought to promote appetite, regarded for its aphrodisiac qualities, and could help to lower blood sugar levels. It is also quite simply very nutritious, and is rich in vitamins and minerals—which makes it a good all-purpose additive to your general diet. Externally, watercress juice was applied as a tonic for abundant, healthy hair, and it was also valued for improving skin quality.

DANDELION An essential in the salads made by both my grandmothers, it was also added to wines and made into coffee substitutes. A thoroughly beneficial herb, it can be added to your diet in any way—to eat or drink—and it will flush the kidneys, help with liver complaints, purify the blood, aid digestion, act as a mild laxative or tonic, improve appetite, and probably relieve symptoms of rheumatism and arthritis. The expressed sap was once a valued treatment for warts. Drinking dandelion coffee late at night may give

rise to the effect, implied by the French common name for this plant, *pissenlit* (piss in bed), so be careful.

NASTURTIUM Leaves, seeds, and flowers are all valued for their tonic effects. Add the leaves and flowers to sandwiches for a lovely peppery taste, similar to watercress, and discover whether they have a positive effect on your skin, hair, nails, and eyes. The seeds are a natural antibiotic which functions without disturbing the intestinal flora, so they are useful for countering food poisoning or the onset of colds and flu. Like watercress, nasturtium flowers, leaves, and seeds can be used to make a strong tonic which will nourish the hair follicles and may help in preventing baldness.

WILD STRAWBERRY This was long regarded as a magic plant, and scientific research is now able to confirm many of the wild strawberry's traditionally esteemed properties. Fruits, leaves, and seeds can all be used, and have diuretic and antiseptic properties. The fruits are high in iron and potassium, so they are nutritious as well as palliative. They soothe chapped and sunburned skin and help to calm an overtaxed liver.

FRENCH ROSE (*Rosa gallica*) Forever associated with life and love, the *Rosa gallica* has a myriad medicinal uses, and is also delicious added to ordinary foods to improve their appeal to the senses, mind, and body. Cakes, jams, ice creams, candies, wines, and salads will all gain from the addition of *R. gallica* petals (remove the white bit at the base, which has a slightly bitter

taste); crushed petals—and of course the hips in fall—form the basis of a syrup for coughs and chest complaints. A decoction made by adding plenty of rose petals to boiling water (about 1 quart) and infusing for ten minutes will produce an excellent tonic for the old and young; it is also useful for anyone who has just finished a course of antibiotics, as it re-establishes the intestinal flora. And, of course, it will always cheer the spirits to see roses added to anything.

GARLIC If you don't find this bulb unpleasant, let it form the basis of a healthy diet. A powerful antiseptic and antibiotic, it is an excellent general tonic, promotes appetite, can be used to treat diarrhea, nausea, and stomach cramps; is good for the circulatory system (and therefore, the heart); and relieves cold and flu symptoms. Along with onions, it reduces blood pressure, aids digestion, eliminates toxins from the system, and regulates all the vital organs, including the blood sugar level. Use fresh bulbs, as prolonged storage reduces the impact of the plant. And, if the smell really offends you, try chewing copious quantities of parsley to counteract this.

PARSLEY Not to be taken by pregnant women. This herb has legendary powers to counter the strong smells of garlic and onions, freshens the breath, disguises drinking, and is said to be an aphrodisiac. It also aids digestion, eases flatulence, and, with a high vitamin C and iron content, is a good tonic and additive to salads. The expressed juice treats bruises as well as ear- and toothache.

CILANTRO (CORIANDER)
A stimulant herb, coriander is prized as an aphrodisiac and believed to combat fatigue and apathy. The Chinese have long regarded it as the bestower of immortality. The seeds have a mildly narcotic effect, are sedative, and ease headache, tension, and nervous exhaustion.

CHERVIL Valued since the Middle Ages for its medicinal properties, this pleasant-tasting herb is diuretic, cleanses the liver and kidneys, and was used to bathe women in after they had given birth—possibly because of its reputation for dissolving blood clots. Today it is still used as a mild but effective eyewash (boil 2 oz. of fresh leaves in a quart of water, strain, cool, and use as a compress for those suffering tired or inflamed eyes, or for the treatment of styes). Added to salads, the leaves provide extra flavor and are a good general tonic.

ROSEMARY The most famous ingredient in many an elixir of youth, rosemary is certainly a cardio-tonic, stimulant herb which works as an antiseptic, diuretic, and antispasmodic. A mild infusion (like a light tea), made from flowering tips and leaves, is a good tonic for convalescents and anyone suffering depression or anxiety. As a stronger tonic for external bathing, the herb treats bruises, sprains, and blisters and helps to heal wounds. It also seems to have a stimulating effect on the brain and memory.

CALENDULA This lovely herb, whose petals look delightful in salads or soups, reduces fevers, soothes intestinal disorders, is antiseptic and antifungal, and helps to heal skin problems. It is also used as a rinse for the hair, to lighten it. My grandmother swore by it, taken for a week before menstruation to ease the pain and PMS (as we would now say) and to regularize the cycle altogether. It is also used as a wash for eczema, burns, and bruises.

LAVENDER The medicinal properties long ascribed to lavender have now been backed up by modern research. This sedative, tranquilizing herb has been used for centuries to counter insomnia, headache, nervous stress, fever, flu, and other respiratory disorders, and externally—as a compress or bath—to treat burns and bacterial skin problems. Nowadays the oil replaces the need for making strong decoctions, and just a drop used neat on a burn or bite will speed healing and ease the pain. This essential herb may assist in the prevention of hair loss, eases rheumatic complaints, and helps cell renewal. The flavor of lavender is also inspirational in cakes, jellies, ice creams, and fish or meat dishes. A must for the senses as well as for the first aid kit.

HOPS have long been valued for their aromatic, preserving qualities, as well as their general tonic effect. In a nonalcoholic form (an infusion can be made from crumbled cones), hops are sedative and calming, aid the digestive process, counter irritation and insomnia, and soothe headache. The young shoots may be eaten, lightly steamed, like asparagus.

MEADOWSWEET The favorite herb of Queen Elizabeth 1, this plant was held sacred by the Druids, as it made the heart glad and was a general analgesic; indeed, it does contain salicylic acid and thus eases pain in much the way that aspirin does. Steeped in beer and wine, it makes a delicious, heady brew; and as a weak tea it may help with the elimination of cellulitis. Its delicious perfume made it a favorite strewing herb in Elizabethan times.

LEMON BALM (*Melissa*) Paracelsus deemed it the reviver of the spirits, and this wonderful herb is another essential in the witches' pantry. The sedative properties make it a good ingredient in herb pillows, but the antispasmodic properties also render it a good de-stressing herb, ideal for women who are tense and premenstrual. In fact, lemon balm is highly regarded as a gentle aphrodisiac, as it calms the nerves and lifts the spirits. The leaves are wonderful added to sandwiches and salads, omelettes, or fish dishes; it also adds a tangy lemon flavor to candies and cakes. It is an ideal general tonic and is easily grown, even, in mild climates, throughout winter. Make a tea (infusing 1 oz. of fresh leaves in 2 cups boiled water for five minutes); sweetened with honey, it could promote longevity.

EVENING PRIMROSE A herb now much in vogue, evening primrose has been used since the seventeenth century in Europe in a syrup form to counter asthma and heavy, chesty coughs. It also has gastrointestinal uses, and is now valued for its gammalinoleic acid, which the body uses to produce prostaglandins. This helps to maintain and replenish healthy tissue and promote a sense of well-being. The expressed oil (most easily bought in capsule form) may help in the prevention of heart problems and menstrual tension, as well as improving skin and nail condition. Much has been said about its capacity to balance too much alcohol consumption—taken in a decent quantity just before bed, it may indeed reduce the effects of a hangover.

VIOLET Granny's best saved for last. This sweetly fragrant, fragile-looking flower was beloved of the Greeks and Romans, and also by the Emperor Napoleon. It conferred fertility, was requisite in love potions, and made a delicious, fragrant wine. Valued for treating headache, migraine, insomnia, and nervous tension, it contains the glycoside of salicylic acid (aspirin again), and the leaves and flowers are mildly laxative. Tea, or a stronger syrup, brewed from the leaves will aid the treatment of coughs and colds, which is why it is sometimes available as a throat pastille. Violets were popularly believed to help cure cancer, but more tests need to be carried out to verify this claim. Use the flowers—leaves too—in cakes and salads, and enjoy the aroma they release as you dine.

USING HERBS

Every day, fill a large salad bowl with as many herbal leaves and flowers from this list as you can manage. Spread the good practice by inviting a friend over for lunch to talk through and ease problems. The release of difficulties is vital to daily well-being, for problems hung on to are ultimately the cause of many serious health problems.

Make compresses, and muslin herb bags for use in the bath, when the spirits are under attack, drawing information and inspiration from the plants listed. Choose an appropriate moment to boost your psychological and physical self-healing before things get out of hand.

THE RAINBOW OF SCENT. A different, soothing oil should be placed in every room and in the office: this is the "rainbow of scent." The scents listed include a balance of low, middle, and high notes (speaking "perfumely,") and help to balance your mood and sensitivity. If you are too sensitive, little things inflame your emotions. If you are insensitive, you cannot respond warmly to the needs of those closest to you. BALANCE IS ALL.

Some scents can be blended for perfect harmony. To counter general anxiety—the root of most poor health—blend 10 drops each of Roman chamomile, lavender, and sandalwood in 1 fl. oz. of base oil for bathing, and massage, or disperse in equal amounts in a burner.

For nervous exhaustion—especially if it is emotionally inspired—balance 10 drops each of rose attar, geranium, and sandalwood, and use as above. Massage is the best method of dealing with this problem—so you need a friend to minister to you, or vice versa. If you feel yourself reaching a serious state of tension, seek professional counseling; but it will also help to burn a predominantly rose attar-lavender scent combination in your work and home area. A few days off, with plenty of restful sounds and scents, may be enough to bring the situation back under control; but strike as soon as you feel under stress.

Lavender, frankincense, and marjoram in equal amounts, and dealt with as above, will help you to counter a growing sense of panic. Peppermint and grapefruit will help you deal with fatigue and mental apathy—blend with lavender or marjoram if you simply feel mentally debilitated.

The basis of personal beauty—and projecting the best you have—is to feel a sense of your own self-worth. Contentment and joy radiate from within, showing on the outside. So, to look your best on the outside, work on the inside. Including the herbs listed on pages 176–8 in your diet will help hugely—giving you energy, good skin, and radiant health. The rainbow of scent will contribute to beauty, too. Hyacinth, rose, and sandalwood will improve your feelings about yourself—the start of looking good. Jasmine, patchouli, and orris make us joyful—and this helps us to radiate beauty to others. Make these blends part of your daily routine. Equal amounts can be blended together to produce a wonderful fragrance, which can be misted into the air by way of a plant spray bottle; add the oils to clear spring water, and mist it into the room where you are working, or onto fabric to carry for a little longer. Spray some on your hair after shampooing and conditioning—for scent remains longest on your hair.

MUSIC

Music is also important to health and resilience. Sounds heal us. Musical notes are a vibratory force which combine to emit a color all their own, and these colors speak directly to our souls and hearts. Always work with music that lifts you; and when working magic, surround yourself with music that has a soothing, uplifting, vitalizing, emotionally charged impact to suit the subject matter of whatever you are working on.

MASTER SPELL: **FOR GOOD HEALTH.** This spell uses a small marble statue with ivy bound around the brow (you could use an existing one from your garden, or another outside statue, just as easily as a small portable bust-size one); you will design a pentagram (five-pointed star) from forest-green ribbon; and a single candle will burn next to it, also in deep forest-green.

There are no variations: this one spell can be used for any health problem, and for any person. Use it to drive away the first signs of bad health, or to work a spell for generally attracting good health, or for working a vigil while someone else is ill.

YOU WILL NEED

Ivy; a small statue (as above); 1¹/₂ yards of deep forest-green ribbon; a small piece of handmade paper, scented with the oil (as below); pine, sandalwood, cedarwood, or rosewood oil; a deep forest-green pillar candle.

MOON PHASE: *Waning, if you are driving away bad health; waxing, if you are trying to attract lasting good health*

Start by choosing your music: a Gregorian chant or other ecclesiastical music is very soothing and creates serenity, but use whatever makes you feel comfortable. Secure the ivy around the brow of the statue with a small bow cut from the green ribbon, and sing a song of enchantment and serenity as you bind it. Then write your name, or that of the ill person you are helping, on a slip of handmade paper, which you have first impregnated with one of the oils above—or you can select your own favorite from the "rainbow of scent." It is important to choose a scent you like, for it is to represent your—or your friend's or relative's—healthy, happy, resilient spirit. Scent the paper by placing it

in a drawer or box containing scented absorbent cotton, and leave it overnight. Handmade paper is usually very porous and will take on the scent easily. Tuck the paper underneath the statue.

Now make up a five-pointed star from the green ribbon: each side should be about 10–12 inches long. Place the pillar candle to one side of the star—or if you prefer, put it in the center. Touch the ivy and the statue, caressing the head, and then light the candle; whisper a prayer-wish for, as Keats said, *"Sweet dreams, and health, and quiet breathing."* "Breathe in" the green from the ribbon and the candle; take it right into your system, and imagine green vitality, resilience, longevity. See yourself or the person you are helping like a tree in spring, sprouting blossoms of new life after the low ebb of winter.

Be thoroughly peaceful, and let the candle burn for about an hour. Concentrate from time to time on the brow of the statue and your name underneath, seeing strength entering the pores of your body and the depth of your soul. Think a little of anyone else who needs bolstering in this way, and envision them growing stronger too. Breathe in the fragrance from the oil on the paper—if you slip it out to inhale the scent, slip it back again.

Repeat this procedure two or three times more over the next few days, then treasure up the ivy and tie it around the slip of paper like a scroll. Seal it finally with a few drops of the green wax, then put it somewhere safe.

HOME AND HEARTH

THE

REED MOON COINCIDES IN THE NORTHERN

HEMISPHERE WITH THAT PERIOD OF EARLY NOVEMBER

WHEN THE WINTER IS COMING ON SWIFTLY AND WE THINK OF THE

HEARTH—LIGHTING THE FIRES—AT HOME. THIS ALSO IS THE MOMENT

WHEN LARGE BONFIRES ARE LIT OUTSIDE. AT THIS TIME, TRY TO HAVE A FIRE LIT

IN SOME WAY WITHIN YOUR DOMESTIC ENVIRONMENT. THIS COULD TAKE THE FORM

OF A CANDLE, BUT IT IS WONDERFUL IF YOU CAN MANAGE A SMALL OPEN FIRE. THE

REED'S CLOSEST ASSOCIATION WITH THE HOME WAS ITS USE AS FUEL, IN RUSH MATTING ON

THE FLOOR AND, MOST IMPORTANTLY, FOR THATCHING. IT HAS COME TO SYMBOLIZE HOME

LIFE FOR THE PURPOSES OF MAGIC—AND MOST ESPECIALLY, IT IS THE MOON AND "TREE"

MOST CONCERNED WITH PROTECTION. THUS, ANY SPELL FOR BLESSINGS ON YOUR HOME—

OR MAGIC WORKED TO PROTECT YOUR HOME OR ATTRACT A NEW ONE—SHOULD BE

DONE NOW. HERE WE EXPLORE WAYS OF HONORING THE SPIRITS OF THE HOME

AND DECORATING YOUR HOUSE TO IMPROVE YOUR HEALTH, PROSPERITY,

AND HAPPINESS: A SORT OF WITCHES' FENG SHUI. THE RIGHT

CHOICES OF COLOR AND DESIGN COULD ENHANCE YOUR

WHOLE FUTURE WAY OF LIVING.

REED MOON—MOON OF HOME AND HEARTH. Color: WHITE (overlaid with a tapestry of other colors to adjust mood and need within the home). Scents: BASIL (sanctity), JASMINE (luxury), MELISSA (female), PINE (male), TUBEROSE (joy). Number: 12. Now is the moment for recharging ourselves, and this chapter concerns the space in which to do it. THIS IS WHERE WE FOCUS ON THE LOVE OF THE HOME.

"'Piper sit thee down and write
In a book that all may read.'
So he vanished from my sight
And I plucked a hollow reed."
FROM THE INTRODUCTION TO
"SONGS OF INNOCENCE"
WILLIAM BLAKE

In the American "log-cabin pattern" quilt, the fiery red patch at the center of the block symbolizes the "home fires burning"—which was formerly, as now, indicative of someone to come home to. All that follows is about the life force of the home itself and how to ensure a happy, blessed dwelling.

A part of your home must always remain sacred. There is an old tradition of constructing an altar, not just for the purposes of your magic making, but also because it is thought essential to invite the world at large—and the deity therein—into your own home to create a microcosm of the blessed realm: "As above, so below." Thus you should have a designated space that is your permanent altar—a small area set aside in which nothing material or functional is to occur except your thanks, and spell-prayers, being offered up: A PLACE OF CALM.

However, various aspects of your home should be altars to different ends. Your bedroom should be an altar to rest and peace, as well as to love. Your kitchen should be an altar to health and hospitality. Your bathroom should be an altar to health and purity; your office to wisdom and higher thought, as well as material success. Your "HEARTH" room—the heart of the home, or living room—should be an altar to the love of all beings.

CREATING THE ALTAR OF THE BLESSED HOUSE
Your home should contain one small space that enacts, physically, a prayer for blessings within your home and family existence there. It should include emblems strong enough to exude a powerful, magnetic pull on positive energy, which will be enticed to take up residence with you. This small area was customarily in the room of the fire—the living area where all the family gathered for strength; so you must designate a little table or windowsill, or a space beside a fireplace, if you have one, in which to lay out your pictorial message to the deity.

A BEEHIVE is the witches' symbol for happy, harmonious home life—everyone dwelling together making a honeyed existence. Also, a SHELL, which signifies an exotic home, is especially symbolic of hopes of going somewhere special and dwelling in a romantic, dream home. This is partly because shells come from water, the element of emotion. To create an altar to the deity for your strong wish of dwelling within a supportive, romantic, peaceful abode, draw upon these symbols in any combination you feel comfortable with, and create a signature altar. You might, for example, use beeswax candles and replenish them on a regular basis; or you might find a simple honey-fragranced candle next to which you might place a small silver or jeweled bee. Some companies actually make a beehive candle; or you might find another way to represent a "honeyed home" that is personal to you. I have a beautiful African basket containing nautilus shells on my altar, to keep a prayer lit for those dear to me who live thousands of miles away: part of my home is in the English countryside, and part in sunny Sydney, where my mother and sister and some friends live. The shells, alongside my candles, link me to both homes.

If you feel your home has been under siege from negative or unhappy people who perhaps have visited or stayed, walk through each day with some incense to cleanse the area, and leave it burning on your altar next to the candles, shells, or whatever you have chosen. It is good to do this even if you know you yourself have been stressed more than usual; OUR HOMES ARE OUR SHELLS, AND SOMETIMES THEY NEED STRENGTHENING.

OTHER ALTARS

It is valid to create support altars in separate spaces. A bedroom should contain an "ALTAR TO LOVE," incorporating colors and emblems from the chapter on LOVE (pages 42-51). Place a shell there, too, if your partner is a foreigner, or loves the sea—or if you do. Place a growing plant there if you want to show that your love continues to grow and learn. The kitchen will have, perhaps, A HERBAL ALTAR, where potted herbs or related plants are grown, which can become the focus of some kitchen candles,

and colors, ribbons and/or emblems drawn from the chapter on HEALTH (pages 172-183). If you are preparing a feast for a special occasion, incorporate some additional material in your "kitchen altar" from the suggestions in the CELEBRATION chapter (pages 144-157).

Near your front door or in your entrance hall, your altar will be simple but could contain, besides the candle, an acorn or oak leaf. Your reference points will be drawn from the chapter on SECURITY (pages 98-107). Perhaps burn some frankincense or sandalwood incense near your door to welcome people and attune them to your positivity. In other words, you are asking your guests' subconscious minds to leave their doubts and angers at the door as they come in.

Your study, office, or desk area will be dedicated to either WISDOM (pages 132-143) or WORK (pages 66-75), or both. If you are an artist, you might draw on some ideas from the chapter on VISION (pages 32-41). If you are an excellent starter of projects but not always a finisher, try adding in some colors and thoughts from the chapter on COMPLETION (pages 196-207), to ensure that you get to the end of your work. Again, decide on the combination of pictograms and symbols, colors and scents that appeal to you from the suggestions given, and make them personal to you in some way, so that you can read the ideas you have woven into your environment and be reminded of their function for you.

To sum up, the idea of constructing the altars is based on similarities. Your altar is a microcosm of sympathetic elements drawn together, peacefully and aesthetically, to enact a strong psychological message of harmony, strength, joy, and so on. Your thoughts make the connection between the existing miniature "theater" of your altar and your own home and life. It is that simple, and very effective. Your wishes are the key: wish strongly, and you will have an impact on the real world around you.

DECORATING YOUR HOUSE: A Wiccan Feng Shui. The elements of fire, earth, air, and water are vital to the components of magic and worship: we are grateful for all of them in our lives and honor them in magic. All must be placed somewhere in your home to draw into it the requisite elements of a good, balanced life.

Although the most obvious principal element of this chapter is fire, water is also significant, because it was believed that fire and water were the two most important elements of creation. Thus, in "feng shui for witches," these two elements must be in balance everywhere.

THE BEDROOM

This should contain all the elements, to rebalance the renewing soul during rest. Hence the advice regarding the altar, where a plant growing in a pot, basket, or window box will symbolize life on earth and place the all-important symbolic element of our planetary home close to our resting souls. Always have a growing plant in your bedroom, as well as on your main "HEARTH" altar. Choose a cyclamen, traditionally, if you want the plant to do the job of adding protection to your home, plus roses, pansies, peonies, or any combination of the three, for pure love.

Flowers in glass (which has come through fire) filled with water, and flowers placed in a metal vase (for metal comes through both fire and earth) will combine the elements of emotion (water), passion (fire), and good sense (metal/earth). A window opened for at least half an hour every day, even in winter, admitting air, will make the vital link with this element. Air also symbolizes the medium of our carried thoughts and prayers, so it is essential to open a window for a moment in the morning, to send your dreams into the real world outside.

A mirror is vital for bouncing thoughts on: bad ones away from you, good ones toward you. There should always be two mirrors in the bedroom (as well as two in the bathroom, a large one near the front door, and two in your main living area—though one of them might not necessarily be seen), and it is lucky to place colored pouches behind them. Have a pink pouch filled with roses and lavender for reflecting romantic and passionate love, and another of your own choice of color and content, depending on what you feel is most lacking in your life. It might be material strength, luck, knowledge, protection. Go back to the appropriate chapter and decide what is required most for you. Placing the representative herb/flower, color, and scent in a pouch tied behind the mirror will place that dream in your dream world, and bring it closer to reality.

Candles must abound in the bedroom, as everywhere. Choose colors for love and sex in your bedroom, scent them, and play massage games by candlelight. This not only is romantic (disguising our imperfections by softer light) but also carries the element of passion as we touch each other. If you have a fireplace in your bedroom, put a candle near this; if not, find an appropriate home for this all-important medium of love.

In the past, herbs were always strewn in the house and especially in the bedroom. This was mainly to counteract the really unsanitary smells and conditions we would now find intolerable, but it is still magical to step on herbs and release their odor as well as their properties. If you live in a warm climate and don't have a carpeted floor, you could strew a few fresh herbs on the floor to create a cloud of heady possibilities in your bedroom—as indeed in any room (the bathroom and living area respond well to this). Traditional choices are lady's bedstraw, sweet woodruff, violet, lavender, peony, and clary. Inevitably, it is difficult to find these herbs fresh throughout the year unless you grow them, but it is well worthwhile making your own herb pillow from fresh plants you have ordered from a specialist supplier. Add in the flowers of various tranquilizing herbs to give you a restful night's sleep: lavender is relaxing, but also intoxicates the sensual zones; lilac is very soothing and also drowses tensions away; evening primrose will counteract inebriation—so is terrific if you've had a few too many. If you have overeaten, try chamomile and fennel in a pillow, as an herb tea in a special bedtime set, or crushed under your feet before bed; jasmine and honeysuckle flowers are a straight choice for sexual enticement. Every couple of weeks, you could cram a selection of these herbs, chosen for their individual properties, into a muslin bag tied with ribbon.

For lovemaking, specifically, nothing will improve upon scented candles floating hedonistically in beautiful glass bowls. The best fragrances are, again, honeysuckle, bluebell or hyacinth, jasmine, and vanilla. Floating them—with a few small fresh flowers—in reflective glass bowls filled with water will introduce the elements of fire, earth, and water, and create beautiful light illusions and an air redolent of exquisite sensuality. This can also be achieved through mixing your own essential oil combination, put into a base of pure spring water, which you then spritz onto your pillows. I have a small plant spray bottle into which I put clear spring water and add fresh oils each week: vetiver, lemongrass, and sandalwood for sleep; lavender and geranium, rose attar, and tuberose for more active evenings. Benefits are

mutual: you will thank yourself, and be thanked. Moreover, you have taken the trouble to achieve something out of the ordinary, especially if you vary your scents and color combinations regularly.

And finally, ribbons and music. Tie the former into clouds above you, as representative wishes for what you want. Create a soft canopy of muslin or other cotton fabric above your head to send your thoughts soaring into the clouds, and tie the corners with blue ribbons for eternal love, red for passion at the beginning of a love affair, pink for perpetual love, yellow for intellect, green for healing, and each and every color you have learned about throughout this book.

Music is the language of the gods: the very word "enchantment" carries the song of ecstasy—the music of the spheres. Hearing is a primary sense; we need to listen to the sounds of beauty in the world to recreate beauty in our lives. So, arrange music in your sleeping environment, to soothe, to excite, to calm, to ignite. It is far more important than a television set to a magic life. It will feed and support your mind, calm your overstretched senses, create a mood for sexual pleasure, and even lift you into realms of the godlike, uncovering the possibility of genuinely divine intimacy.

THE HEARTH ROOM (OR LIVING ROOM)

Look for the "soul" of the space you principally live in—especially near a fireplace or a special feature that you feel magnetically drawn to. Adorn this area, and give it a special "battery." You may do this by laying out fresh flowers and potted plants or placing candles; but the most important thing is that you must create a "hearth" (literally, the heart of the home), even if it is only a painting of a fire glowing. At the very least, cluster candles of many shapes and sizes together—perhaps in glass jars or divided boxes—and make a space around them. Place a small mirror somewhere near your candlelit hearth to reflect the light and positivity you create here. It need only be small, but find a mirror that fits the mood of your little area, and make sure that the candlelight bounces off it to illuminate the parallel world.

Once you have your "hearth," release aromatics into the air to attract the divine and neutralize pain and anxiety. In many cultures this was done very simply: pinecones and resins formed the center of many a log fire, as did other perfumed woods like cedar and rosewood. To clear the head and attract positive spirits, beautiful herbs and spices were burned on incense burners such as charcoal burners. It is now easy to find these commercially and to buy incense mixture in jars instead of the usual sticks; or you can make up your own blend of precious spices to burn in this same way. Alternatively, place some vaporizing oils next to your hearth.

Traditional scents for the purification and harmonizing of the heart of the home are pine resin and oil and bergamot (for the male element, and thus very important if there is a lack of male energy in your house); melissa, cinnamon, and vanilla (for the female element); rosemary and basil, which can be burned dried or fresh in a fireplace to clear the mind and invite focused thought into your home; benzoin, frankincense, and myrrh, for the deity; and rose and tuberose, for love in the home.

Scent candles with these oils, as a way of dispersing these aromas into the heart and life-pulse of your home. Even carry this benediction into temporary homes: take an appropriately fragranced candle into a vacation house or hotel room, and make gifts of these to friends with whom you are going to stay.

Plants must grow somewhere in your central room, and they must look healthy. These symbolically oxygenate your world, and to do this they should exude color as well as fresh air. Choose plants with blue flowers, plus red or pink, and white or golden yellow. Others may be seasonal options, but these are the

requirements for stability, loyalty, insight, and love. If you want to dedicate one plant to the divine, choose something regal and white, and tie the pot or bucket it is planted in with a white ribbon. My own choice would be a lily (also for the perfume), some jasmine, or an orchid. This invites the highest, noblest spirit into your home.

The scents and plants see to our senses of smell and sight. Touch, hearing, and taste must also be satisfied in our key room. Tactile fabrics and floor surfaces are essential in this one place. As a follower of Wicca thinking and an adept exponent of the craft of magic thought and spell-making, you must pay attention to enhancing all your senses all the time. Thus, bring your feeling capacity into total consciousness in this room, and your other senses will also engage more fully.

Velvet pillows and throws are invaluable in your living room. They bid you to relax, unwind, loosen up, feel good in your own body; they slow you down and turn off anxiety; they welcome others with their message of comfort and luxury. Choose a rainbow of colors, and make them appear and disappear as required: olive green and mulberry, remember, will encourage you to be wise, so place these in an "adult chair," or use them on top of other colors when you feel a call to be especially together mentally. Go to reds if you are initiating something in your living room area, and pinks and lavenders for love. Tactile rugs have the same function: they, too, can be changed around seasonally according to your color needs—but always lift your physical senses with fabric furnishings that, literally, turn you on.

Remember that tiled and ceramic surfaces signal your senses to a different kind of touch: an interplay of stone and brick, tile, and wood will keep you alert and ensure that your senses are constantly alive. This is all the more true if you pad through your home in very soft shoes, or bare feet.

Sound is—for me, clairaudient since childhood—the most important sense to satisfy in this central room of the happy home. I can live without trips abroad, but never without good sound equipment and a wonderfully varied collection of music to soothe my nerves and encourage my soul to yearn for something better.

Chanting, as I have said, is the key to magic at the highest level; it enters your being on the vibratory airwaves and is the channel to the soul. Words spoken have a magic property; sound travels through time. Chanting also induces a meditative state by virtue of its repetition, and is fundamental to all prayer; but you do not have to play a Gregorian chant to induce your own level of religious being. Play any music that makes your soul happy: then send transcendental thought through the ether.

Sound should surround you—so organize your equipment, insofar as possible, to achieve this, with speakers in balanced corners of your hearth room. Never allow negative or ugly sound into your hearth room for long; these vibratory waves have a lingering effect of melancholy, so balance your amount of Mahler, or songs of heartbreak, or heavy metal, with sounds of pure harmonious glory. When spell-making, try the exercise of sending thoughts to another soul while listening to music you know you both like. The music waves should deepen your focus and recall of the other person.

Taste ought to be catered for in any way possible—but unobtrusively in this area. The throne of taste is the kitchen, but here, by the hearth, have a small bowl of nuts, olives, or candies to entice the taste buds and offer something in this department. A large bowl of colorfully wrapped chocolates will almost always have your visitors (and you) salivating. Quality is the essence—not quantity. A yoga teacher I know in Sydney always has a handful of smoked almonds in his living room with which to welcome his guests; and nuts are traditionally a blessing from the gods.

And finally, the sixth sense. How could we leave out this unquantified element? Your main living area might show some reference (as veiled as you like) to the spiritual realm and the gift of extra sight and power you wish to find within. Discreetly, put a pentagram—a five-pointed star—in your hearth room. It could simply take the form of a leftover Christmas star if you want to be mysterious, but it is lovely to tape out a little pentagram in colored ribbon: white, yellow, red, blue, purple. Make it tiny, but utter all of your general prayers over the pentagram, and light a candle in the center.

Ribbons, glassware, crystals, bells and chimes, and symbolic items can be chosen entirely from your own guidance on the subject: this is your home, and should meet your needs and taste. Take inspiration, perhaps, from the ideas in some of the earlier chapters, but always be guided by your own ultimate inclination—for it will be right for you.

A MAGICAL KITCHEN

This does not begin with a shopping list for cauldrons or a witches' broom, though have these if you like. Kitchens begin with the host's feeling of hospitality and magic radiated to the world. The food you prepare here will have the power to change people who eat with you—so integrity and good hygiene are the key points.

Always have at least one growing herb to symbolize growing health in the area of nourishment. A potted supermarket plant, replaced weekly, is better than nothing; and a window box of seeds lovingly planted by you, herbs growing cheek by jowl with flowering ornamentals, is the best kitchen positivity I can think of. Again, have a tiny mirror above your cooking place to send packing gremlins who would spoil your food—never bake a cake without this fail-safe.

A well-lit kitchen is also much desired by the witchy cook, and is sometimes a problem for those dwelling in a small space where a kitchen has been carved out of no space at all. Try to ameliorate this with good lighting: light and sunshine are the first ingredients of positivity that you want to incorporate into your cooking, to create sunshiny characters at your table. Is this why such extraordinary hospitality is inherent in the people of Mediterranean lands?

Remember candles in the kitchen: light and prayer are as important here as anywhere else in the house.

THE STUDY

An important area for many, as it is the place of serious thought and perhaps material stability, the study/office deserves a short entry of its own.

Tie many things in clusters with ribbons. Books tied with ribbons will celebrate knowledge and symbolize what there is still to learn. A dish of water, in a wood or metal bowl, should be near your working and living spaces. This also adds moisture back into the rooms when winter heat takes it from the air.

Counteract the impersonal effect of electronic equipment: if you have PCs, fax machines, printers, and other computerized elements in your work space, offset these with plants, goldfish, or photographs of people you love, in order to introduce a human element. Go to work on herb pillows and ribbons to introduce feeling and scent into what might otherwise be a sterile atmosphere. Grow one luxury plant, with a coin pushed into the soil, for certainty of perpetuating your work and cash in the future. An orchid, jade plant, or any small fruiting tree will be symbolic of the fruits of labor and fertility.

AND GENERALLY . . .

These are thoughts to consider when energizing your whole house to a positive existence.

- MIRRORS can be placed in the hall or near the front door (to reflect back the quality of thought sent to you, to re-bless those who send you love and fend off those who send you thorns), and in the bathroom, not only for practical reasons, but also to aid you in your quest for personal health and beauty. A bathroom mirror should be an object of beauty itself, and should be carefully chosen to reflect you at your best. Cheap mirrors will fail to do this, and may send you off into the world grumpy, dejected, and lacking confidence.

- CANDLES should abound—everywhere. They are your link with past, present, and future, your thoughts sent into the atmosphere, and your hopes borne aloft. Buy the best you can afford, and replace them as they are used up. Ask for candles as presents from friends: a candle given has special value.

- SCENT your home with lavender and other healing/balancing scents. Every room should have a scented oil burner, which can disseminate a different mood-scent in each place.

- Make something at the fire on a regular basis: toasting bread is an age-old symbol of the daily grain renewed by fire— and it is delicious. The same can be done with chestnuts, marshmallows, or even pinecones and other woods for scent.

MASTER SPELL: **TO BLESS YOUR DWELLING.** This spell is based around a white seashell; it uses a beautiful key from one of the locks in your door, next to the seashell, and the magic must be worked at some kind of fireplace. (There are no candles in this spell—just a fire.)

YOU WILL NEED

5 white ribbons, each 12 inches long; a fireplace (any open fire, such as a barbecue, will do if there really is nothing better); a perfect white conch or nautilus seashell; a key from the prettiest lock in your house (if you have only one door, get a special key cut and have it silverplated for this spell); benzoin incense; a pinecone; a small piece of paper on which to write your address.

MOON PHASE: *Full*

Deep-breathe on the full moon: draw the light right into your soul. Lay out the five lengths of ribbon into a five-pointed star, which you will place before the hearth or fireplace. In the center of the star, place the shell. Now take your key, offer it for blessing to the moon, and make a prayer over it that the inhabitants of the house, and the events that occur within it, will be blessed with luck and light, goodness and wisdom. Ask, too, for wisdom within your own domain: in other words, that decisions you make within your home will be the right ones. Lay the key beside the shell, and wish for a happy, romantic home.

Light the fire and burn some of the benzoin incense and pinecones in it; waft the scents through the space you are working in, and across the nearby shell and key.

Finally, write your address on a small piece of paper, purify it in the scented smoke, and ask particularly for protection from fire and tempest. Wish hard for several moments for a truly sound domestic life—for simple blessings on your home; then burn the paper completely in the fire.

The spell is complete as the fire burns low; but keep the shell and key for an altar in your home, and light a candle by them regularly.

THE ONLY VARIATION IS FOR A NEW HOME.

Before you move into a new dwelling, put ribbon (forest-green, or cherry-pink if it is a house you are moving into with a lover—or both together) across the door, and cut it, both of you together, with new scissors. Then perform the spell as above, placing the new scissors in conjunction with the shell and the key. Keep the ribbon tied near the door ever after.

COMPLETION

ELDER MOON

OUR

YEAR IS DRAWING TO AN END; IT IS TIME

FOR US TO GIVE BACK TO THE SPIRIT OF THE WORLD. WE

ARRIVE FULL CIRCLE AT THE 13TH MOON MONTH, THE ELDER MOON,

MOON OF COMPLETION, COVERING LATE NOVEMBER TO LATE DECEMBER.

THIS IS A CHAPTER OF MANY BLESSINGS—THE FINISHING TOUCH TO ALL MAGIC,

FOR FULLEST POWER. MUCH OF THIS CONCERNS SAYING "THANK YOU" WHEN MAGIC

MAKING HAS PRODUCED GOOD EFFECT. ONCE YOUR WISH HAS BEEN GRANTED, IT IS

GOOD MANNERS TO THANK THE POWERS THAT BE FOR TURNING YOUR MENTAL STRENGTH

INTO MATERIAL MANIFESTATION. "BLESSINGS" MIGHT INCLUDE THE EXTRAS IN LIFE, SUCH

AS MONEY SUPERFLUOUS TO REAL REQUIREMENTS, AN EXTRA CHILD, OR SOME OTHER

ADDITIONAL BOUNTY. MAGIC MAKING INCLUDES ADVICE FOR "LETTING GO"—EITHER OF

A PARTNER AFTER SEPARATION, TO KEEP IT AMICABLE, OR OF A RELATIVE OR FRIEND

WHO "GOES AWAY," PERHAPS EVEN TO DIE. ALL THINGS HAVE THEIR TIME AND

PLACE, AND THIS KIND OF MAGIC IS AS IMPORTANT AS ANY OTHER. WE

RECOGNIZE THE CYCLE OF DEATH AND REBIRTH: AFTER THIS, ALL

LIFE'S LESSONS HAVE BEEN LEARNT, AND SHOULD BE

PRACTICED FOR THE BENEFIT OF ALL.

ELDER MOON—MOON OF COMPLETION AND WHOLENESS. Color: GOLD. Scents: ORANGE, NEROLI, BERGAMOT, CITRUS, ROSE, PINE. Number: 13.

This last moon in the year, which falls across the period of Yule, is governed by the beautiful wintry elder moon, which rules magic of completeness, wholeness, new cycles, and rebirth.

"Weave a circle round him thrice,
And close your eyes with holy dread,
For he on honey-dew hath fed,
And drunk the milk of Paradise."
"KUBLA KHAN"
SAMUEL TAYLOR COLERIDGE

The hollow stem of elder, with the pith scooped out, was used to rekindle fires and make them burn hotter—literally, to give life to a dying fire—and it has always been closely associated with witchcraft and magic. It was believed that a dryad, or tree nymph, dwelled within the heart or branches of the tree, so this was not a tree from which to make furniture or to burn carelessly on a fire. This tradition persists among country people today, who may regard the tree as bad luck; its spirit would haunt anyone who abused its soul!

The elder tree is one of the most useful for ailments contracted at this chilly time of year—which is why it was so valuable to witches. Elder has been revered for its medicinal properties forever, and seemingly by all peoples. It appears in the Jewish Kabbala, and was allegedly the tree by which Judas hanged himself (for it is a tree of justice, which demands great respect); in some traditions Christ's cross on Calvary was made from it. Certainly, country people may still be observed doffing their caps to the Elder Mother to beg her good grace, and her protective powers are sought in the afterlife: branches were once buried with the dead to protect them from evil spirits on their last journey! Thus, too, the elder tree and moon make the final journey in the dying year, to ensure rebirth (the close connection here with the Christmas "birth" celebration is clear).

In the past, all parts of the tree were used in healing, but as we are now aware of the toxic properties of the leaves and berries, only the beautiful, sweet-fragranced flowers are generally used, and other parts of the plant should be avoided, although the berries are boiled to make syrups which are powerful remedies against respiratory congestion and coughs. Raw berries and the leaves should never be taken.

The healing elder flowers, which can be cooked up in a variety of ways, help hay fever and asthma sufferers and are a good source of vitamin C, which explains their long history of use as a treatment for colds and to reduce fevers; they make a delicious still or sparkling wine and can be harvested in high summer, then bottled and left to mature. This makes them the perfect toast for a "thank you" for good fortune in the year, under the elder moon, at Yuletide. If you have no access to the flowers—or no time—just add some commercially made elderflower syrup to your own "champagne" or white wine.

THE TREE: Besides being associated with Christmas, the Christmas tree embodies the godly spirit of vegetation and fecundity. During the Roman Saturnalia, pines were brought into the temples by tree-bearers, as the pine was sacred to the goddess; subsequent customs often used a bough from fruit trees instead of pine to decorate the house at Yule, ensuring a fertile year ahead. Placing certain fruit tree branches in water would encourage them to blossom—which was a good sign for the future.

The holly and ivy, which we have talked about in earlier chapters, also found a sacred place at this time of year in the home; the holly was the symbol of the waning year, and at this time the Holly King still has command, until December 21/22, when he joins in battle with the Oak King, who will govern the new growing year. Ivy is a plant of survival and resurrection right through the winter and symbolizes the movement from winter stillness and death to rebirth.

Incorporate all the customs you are familiar with and place them in their magical, Pagan context. This will joyously complete the ritual of a magical year.

THE COLOR GOLD

A color associated with the Christmas season for so long, gold is also the color of total attainment and completion. It is associated with the sun at its zenith, and at this time is a request to entice the sun back to its high power once more. It has connotations of joy and brilliance and associations with fire, and instills pleasure and vibrancy.

Gold is used in all magic of this time, and is connected with completion and seeing things through to the end. Only a speck of it is needed. It is a finishing touch; too much is gaudy, and somewhat greedy. To make the Yuletide altar, and the altar of thanks—or for urging all magic making of the year to its conclusion—just the smallest grain of gold, or a few grains of golden sand, or a tiny piece of golden jewelry placed by a gold candle, will be sufficient to raise a golden spirit of celebration. At any time of the year, gold should be placed next to your altar as a prayer of thanks for your spell working being answered.

Completed work also includes helping out a friend with the working of their magic—but without improper interference. You can burn a simple, small golden candle with their name written underneath to boost their magic working, as a kind of "shadow" of their energy. Do not be tempted to do the whole spell for them: anyone else's magic is their own karma, not yours!

The other important thing to do under this moon, and utilizing the vibrancy of gold, is to "give gold"—even the smallest amount. During this cycle, some gold must leave your hands and benefit others who have less: this is a universal "thank you" for everything. It need only be as much as you can afford—quite literally a few pennies in a collection box. Each time you have to say a "*thanks*" for your magic working well, find a recipient, and give.

For a little bit of magic in everyday life at this time of year, we should employ our magic for the benefit of all on the earth. Spend time strewing flowers on others' paths! Give a tiny bunch of winter violets, or roses, or another flower of color and fragrance, to thank those dear to you just for their friendship. Give plants regularly—tied in shiny paper with a golden bow—for the gift of growth from earth is the finest you can give.

And for a little bit of "completion magic" on your most important concerns, try tying a golden ribbon around the index finger of your dominant hand (left if you are left-handed) and concentrating on the issue itself. Send mental strength to those concerned with you in the affair, and imagine the ending you have worked for being achieved. Concentrate hard and think of a big golden ribbon being tied around the whole matter, with a satisfactory result.

THE SCENTS OF FRUITION AND COMPLETENESS

The oils and fragrances associated with a sense of completeness and the power to carry matters through to the end are, not surprisingly, also connected with the powers of concentration and memory, confidence, and emotional strength. Pine (a very Christmassy scent!) and bergamot, neroli, and rose are the most powerful scents for completion magic and for helping us through obstacles to the winning post.

If you feel your resolve weakening, your mind wandering, or your belief tested in your wish to see something right through to the end; or if you are tired and uncertain that your efforts will ultimately bring the goal you have striven for—this is the moment to work a little everyday magic with these oils and scents.

Bathe in rose or pine oil and breathe in the positive scent. Let your spirits rise with optimism, believe once again that all is within your grasp—that you are indeed nearly there. Fix your thoughts on your desires, and relax on them. Nervous worry is the element most likely to frustrate your work; if you believe truly that you can do something, it will be. This, then, is the "eleventh hour" spell—to convince yourself again at this last moment that all will be well, that your pains have not been in vain. Put aside doubt, and push through to your victory. Tell the spirits and the elements that you are there; lather your body in rose or pine soap, caress and pamper your mind and body, believe in yourself again. Be confident in the strength of your preparation work.

If you are going for a last interview, a final business meeting, a conclusive exam to all that has gone before, a farewell to someone you want to think well of, and they of you: prepare your thoughts and embolden your behavior with orange blossom, neroli, and bergamot scents. Burn a candle scented with one of these, and put your prayer underneath the candle

foot on a piece of paper; concentrate on the matter for a few moments, then blow out your flame. Sally forth in good spirits!

If you are parting from someone you have loved, and wish to remain friendly and be grown up about the split, give them a gift of orange blossom, or mock orange, or a citrus tree, and tie it in beautiful paper fixed with a golden bow. Sincerely wish them happy and well, and you both free of each other in the best ways; your relationship will die away from its old pattern, and a new form of bond will arise—not binding, but warm and imbued with fellow-feeling. This is governed by the elder moon, for it is a death and a rebirth, and shows maturity and humanitarian roundedness.

THE NUMBER 13

In the Tarot, Arcanum XIII is "DEATH," sometimes called "THE REAPER"—which is more truly a symbol of the death or culmination of one set of circumstances paving the way for a brand-new cycle, a new age. It might be termed "The king is dead; long live the king," marking a new growth from the old branch. It is a reminder that we must witness creation, destruction, and then renewal in order to move forward. It is also highly symbolic of the transformation we make as individuals when we release ourselves from material instincts and give our soul to the universal laws of re-creation, and become a more celestial being. This expresses perfectly what we should now know from all the lessons that have gone before, bringing us to a new sense of immortality and freeing us from fetters of all kinds. We should now begin to understand what it is to be complete. THIS, THEN, IS THE WITCHES' NUMBER. LUCKY (NOT UNLUCKY) "13."

THE TASKS OF THE ELDER MOON. The elder moon is certainly about maturity, about slowing your pace a little and thinking roundly and wisely about the whole picture in any given situation. This moon's lesson is one of patience—the patience to see our tasks through to the end—and of tying up loose ends and finishing what we have taken on. Therefore, this is an important time for completing what we have set ourselves, when perhaps we had lost the way, or the impetus, or just forgotten our pledges.

The first gift is, at busy Christmas time, sometimes the hardest to give: time. We are always rushing now, but we should slow down long enough to give those who need us some of our time, even though (or perhaps especially because!) this is often more costly to us than gold. In a hurried and increasingly impersonal world, make a pact to give someone a day of your time with no strings attached. Give time, especially, to your children as a surprise. They will be happier than if you gave them a material gift. Give time to your lover or partner—the more so as your lives are usually very busy. Make time, also, for yourself: put routine and everyday duty aside long enough to think mellow thoughts. Show all those you really love how valued they are—not materially, but emotionally, and with your time.

GIVE TIME TO LETTERS: we never seem to write them anymore, but one of the good things about new technology is how easy it is to keep up a friendship by e-mail. Write someone the smallest of letters—but write it down. The written word is a permanent treasure, and we usually keep those things sent by someone we love. Make this a priority.

Also, revise anything you have written by way of short stories or poetry. If you have outstanding wishes connected with books or publishing, or if you want to submit written material to an agent or magazine, do so now, and with the golden candles and citrus, pine, or rosy scents aiding you. DON'T LEAVE YOUR DREAMS IN THE DRAWER: PUT THEM IN THE MAIL AND WISH THEM WELL!

Then turn your attention to other unfinished business. COMPLETE TASKS: burn oils of orange flower, neroli, citrus, and rose while answering correspondence, complete decorating and painting jobs, do the filing, clear out closets. As this moon coincides with Yule (Christmas), have a little pre-New Year clean-out once a year, and finish old jobs. Throw wasted promises into the wastebasket—and start again. Of course you can't finish everything; but it is important to finish at least one significant thing before the old year ends.

MASTER SPELL: **OF THANKS, AND TO ENSURE COMPLETION OF AN AMBITION.**
This spell is the one to take you through to the happy ending of the fairytale. You
may perform it shortly after doing magic for a particular goal, to tell the entities of
the spirit world that you are confident of return; you may do it if the affair seems
to "drag" a little, and you want to nudge matters along a bit faster; or you can
perform it when your "wish has been granted." Don't forget! It is as important as
remembering to say "thank you" to someone for a lovely gift, and ensures a strong
ongoing relationship. For reasons that will become self-evident, there are again no
true variations. This is another "master number" spell—not an everyday concern!

YOU WILL NEED
A "love-pillow" (see below), which is more than half of this spell;
1 leaf from every tree mentioned in the 13 moons (if you really cannot
manage this, do a drawing in your own hand of the identifiable
shape of each one, using a good source book as your guide);
13 candles of all the colors of the moons (votives or short tapers are
fine); likewise, a "set" of the 13 various ribbons, each 1 yard long;
a photo album with pictures of those dearest to you, and some who
perhaps are not so dear (for forgiveness, which is part of completion).

MOON PHASE: *Any*

MAKING THE "LOVE PILLOW"
This must be an item of your own making, however inept you
think you are at sewing. Make it with love and strong feeling,
and it will be a powerfully woven spell. Using fabric in white
or gold (brocade would also be a good choice), make a pillow
stuffed with herbs, at least some of which have been home
grown. It should be embroidered with threads from all the colors
of the chapters (echoing the ribbons and candles) and sprinkled
with all the scents, but predominantly rose, jasmine, and
lavender. The idea is to embroider a symbolic word or image
that says "thank you" in any form you like. Play music while you
work—and work by lamp- or candlelight. The most successful
pattern might be a simple circle—perhaps consisting of all the
first letters of the names of those who make up your world.
This spell—a piece of "WEAVING"—is your magnum opus.
You should place it near your head and heart at night, and drink
in wisdom, pain, strength, love, thought, and the power to
conclude the things you start. It is the most powerful talisman—
and should be passed on to someone you love when you take
leave of this time and place.

   If you really cannot make your own, buy something
suitable—perhaps a lavender-scented bed pillow in white—and
embroider it yourself with your prayer of thanks, or stuff a small
pillowslip with herbs, embroider a heart or other emblem

(or appliqué one if you prefer) onto it, and secure the open end with a tie made up of all the colored ribbons. It will still be powerful if you do it with care and passion.

THE SPELL PROPER

Make a circle in your main living area with the leaves (or pictures), and the candles tied or encircled with each of the matching ribbons. Sit in the center with your pillow, and the little album or book into which you have placed your photos of the people in your dreams—happy dreams primarily, but those who give you bad dreams too, for these problems should now be released and resolved.

Light the candles and address each color for a moment: look at the red and remember your energy in beginning your tasks; look to the pinky-gold and remember your visions, thinking through what you envisioned your dreams to be; concentrate now on the amber or cherry-pink color, and contemplate your hopes in love; turn your attention to the indigo/blue color, and think about your work duties and aspirations; and so on through all the colors, dwelling on the concerns of each color and the chapters that have gone before, as they affect your life, until you come to the golden candle for this chapter and consider the completion—or the thanks—for which you are making an offering.

Once you have collected all of these (color-coded!) thoughts, bow your head, make your prayer of thanks or final hopes, stroke the album containing those who people your world, and ask for many blessings, and wisdom, and a successful conclusion to your affairs. Let the candles burn down a little: do not hurry this.

After a while, blow out each flame and bow once more. Your tasks are complete.

If you have just a small "thanks" to make, or a very simple wish to nudge the spirits a little to end your affairs according to your hopes, simply embrace and inhale your love pillow, and sleep upon your dreams.

WINTER

As

autumn begins to ebb away, we

are only too aware that the daylight

hours have been shrinking and the earth is

withdrawing into itself. All the energy of the earth's

life force is drawn back into the root systems, and we

must use this season to do the same. We can turn inward,

into our own dream world, to explore our unconscious and

deepest desires, which can then be turned into a stronger reality

in the spring. This is the time to soothe, protect, and heal our

spirit, which often feels sorely tested without the sun's powers

in such full force. This perhaps is why the moment of Yule,

Midwinter Day, when the sun hits its shortest point

and begins to travel back to us again, is psychologically so

important. But for the next few months, in our homes,

gardens, hearts, and spirit, we must make

sure we "wrap up warm." Element: earth.

Direction: north.

THE WINTER SOLSTICE. This is the most important solar event of the year: we are marking the shortest day and the moment of the sun's return. In the north, Midwinter Day is December 21st. In the southern hemisphere it is June 21st.

Yule: the Festival of God—or the sun—marks the "wheel" of the year, from which the word "Yule" is derived. In the Pagan, Celtic past, it was considered very unlucky to turn any wheel on the day of Yule itself. First, one had to await the sun's own return, which meant a day of quiet and rest and honor. These may be the origins of our Christmas break, hardly now a time of peace and quiet! However, this is a time to pause and think over the year, until the first signs of the lengthening day can be witnessed. Then, we should look forward to what may come.

It seems to have parallels across every civilization, and most of the present Christmas traditions can be traced to much older ceremonies, including the star of hope, the sacred candle flames, the decoration of the dwelling with evergreens, Christmas wine or "wassail," the feast, and even gift giving.

The traditional burning of the Yule log ensures good luck for the coming year, but a piece of the log must be carried over until the following Yule. The Christmas candle, also of Pagan origin, was lit every night at the same time from Yule until January 6th to ensure luck and to encourage the return of the fire. As it was lit, the area of most need was uttered over it. Thus, in ritual, breathe a wish of most need—only one—over the candle as you light it from evening to evening. The tallow (or melted wax) should be kept and smeared on any implement of work—originally a plough or spade, but it might now be a pen or computer; this can be made to look pretty, as with sealing wax. You might equally take some of the fire's ash and put it around your winter-sleeping roses—a highly symbolic, but also utterly practical, gesture. Your roses will love it.

Yule rituals can also include some reindeer talismans, so that the horned god (Old Nick or Herne the Hunter) may personally attend your magic. Incorporate evergreens, which symbolize lasting life, into your altar or ritual; and again, create a fire-inspired feast to share with treasured friends or family.

THE WREATH: To celebrate the old way, make a wreath—the symbol of the year turning full cycle, and of no beginning, no end—for the door, with a twig or leaf from every tree, and interlaced with beautiful bright flowers of many colors. The wreath is an expression of faith in the eternity of being; it is also a good symbol of openness and peace, which is complicit with the elder moon. The best wreaths will be made by you, and can in fact be of any material you like. Straw and burlap were sometimes used, as they are sacred to the crops.

GIVING GIFTS: The tradition of presents at this peak moment of the year derives from the belief that, as like begets like, giving generously to others would ensure their goodwill, and would also appease the gods and implore them to favor each person with a generous bounty in the coming year. This aspect of appeasement can also be seen in the offering to St. Nicholas—whereby one would be rewarded generously for one's own generosity!

THE YULE LOG: The real thing was hewn from oak, brought into the hearth with great ceremony, lit from the old fire, and tended to make sure it would not go out for at least the solstice day (December 21). It could be re-lit at sundown each day until the New Year was safely brought in—the whole object being to ensure that the sun would grow again and bring life and warmth. The Yule log was a sacred object, imbued with great magic power, and it was hoped that, from the theory that like begets like, the fire of the sun would surely return. Ashes from the log were later plowed into the fields after the critical "birth" period was over.

Your log could be blessed with your own promise to generate something, according to your gift, that makes the world around you even the tiniest bit better: a witch's pledge. Sprinkle it with your favorite oils or wood shavings for scent, before you set light to it.

THE YULE CANDLES: This was another echo of the sacred flame. It was important to light the candles each night from midwinter to New Year, and the proud flame would ensure abundance in all things. Many items might be laid around the altar of the candle—from money, to food, to wassail. The remnants of the candle were married to the log and burned a last time before the ashes were sown into the soil for fertility. The whole ritual was very phallic and symbolic!

THE YULE FEAST: This, too, echoes the concept that like begets like: if there was a surfeit of food at Yule, the year would ensure plenty to eat! Of course, it was also a pleasure to create a feast to brighten the darkest day of the year, with celebration and light and joy. It was a feast to celebrate the birth of the new growing sun—the most important birthday of the year.

The principal Pagan dish—around which all other feast dishes revolved—was usually a pig, deer, or boar. The boar had an apple in its mouth to genuflect to the goddess (for whom apples were sacred), and the deer was likewise connected with the Green Man and the Holly King, as well as being sacred to the Celtic gods. The famous marriage of venison with juniper berries formed a kind of honorable offering to the cooked animal's spirit and to the gods. Juniper was another important winter herb, for the berries were a huge help against the rheumatic and arthritic illnesses that plagued those who lived in damp, cold, northern winters.

WINTER INCENSE. This is a key time for the burning of incense. Always an aid to meditation and inward thinking, the smoke also recalls the scent of the growing trees and resins, rejuvenating the wintry air with life and magic.

YOU WILL NEED

1/2 teaspoon frankincense; 1/2 teaspoon pine needles; 1/2 teaspoon lemon or orange peel; 1 bay leaf; a tiny slice of cinnamon stick; a few grains of sugar.

Blend your own incense, if you can; otherwise choose ready-made incenses, with which you can work magic and which you can utilize in unusual ways. The resin must make up about half of the mixture. You may choose to add a touch of sugar, which will sweeten the scent and appease the magical spirits, who adore the sweetness in the air. Frankincense is a wonderful choice for scenting linen and bedding as well as rooms, for it adds a blessing to the necessaries of daily life in the winter. A sacred blend would have been three-quarters frankincense and one-quarter myrrh. Blend your ingredients with your mortar and pestle before weighing the quantities.

Blend all the powdered ingredients together, light a carefully insulated charcoal disk, and place your incense on it when the heat has turned it gray-red. Waft the smoke toward your linens and into your dining area. Ask for resilience and triumph over winter ills and seasonal irritations. Very quietly, honor the essence of the sleeping earth. Imagine the incense circling around your home and protecting all that is in it. Stay very calm and quiet, enjoying the scent, while the fragrance lingers—approximately one hour. It will brighten your mood, add confidence and zest, and enhance your mental vigor.

SPELL RIBBONS. There is a very special ritual to be performed with ribbons in winter time, when their color is so important in a brown-gray world.

Purchase some really broad ribbon, about 1 inch wide, in pink for love or blue for luck. Take a contrasting-colored thread and very carefully embroider your name or initials on the ribbon. By early, waxing moonlight, take the ribbon to the prettiest bare tree—one with a perfect shape. Ask la donna della luna (the lady of the moon) in her wintry brightness, the sole luminary of the winter sky, to favor your dearest hopes (in love or in luck) with her magical touch. Tie the ribbon securely into the tree. For the remainder of the moon, wear a stone such as a moonstone or milk opal or a very white diamond, in honor of the moon. Before winter is ended, you will be lucky in your hopes.

CONJURING THE HORN OF PLENTY. This ancient ritual is connected with sunny climes where the grape is part of the staple of economy and joy conjoined. It bears a close resemblance to the wassail ceremony in the north, with the apple trees honored on Twelfth Night Eve. You could perform this if you or a friend have a grapevine growing; otherwise take grapes and a horn of wine yourself, and go into a garden area, enacting this symbolically at any tree. The wine itself should be a pleasure.

THE VINEYARD RITUAL

When you wish for a good harvest, go in winter into the vineyard or wherever vines may grow, on a waxing moon. Look up to the lady of the moon and ask of Diana her help and favor with your future prosperity in this way. Charging your "glass" or horn, toast the moon, saying: "*This is no ordinary wine I drink, but the essence of your life and energies. Diana, spread the vitality of the wine into my vines, and may the grape and my fortunes ripen in the waxing moon. I kiss the hand of the Lady of the Growing Moon, and from this day, until the first bud appears, and the fruit indeed ripens, I ask your blessings on my house. May I draw, in equal measure, profit and pleasure with friends and loved ones.*"

Now, pour a little wine into the ground around the vine or tree, then say: "*I salute here the horns of the moon, with the horn of Bacchus, and promise to balance work and rest-time, responsibility and merriment, in equal proportion.*"

Now you should cast a few grapes around the base of the tree or vine, be still for a few moments, and think of what a "prosperous harvest" means for you individually. Keep some grapes on your main table or at a simple altar for the remainder of the moon, right through the waxing process until it has waned and appeared new. The grapes may be eaten, but must be replaced.

WINTER WARMERS. The prime effort of magical endeavor at this time is to bring into our territory reminders of the still-pulsing life force, so that we can keep our low batteries charged just enough for survival and to spur our mood up to a higher point.

This was the reason behind bringing in evergreens to the house and the table. Pine, mistletoe, ivy, and holly, which had such a significant magical ritual function throughout the seasons, are now called upon to impart their message of strength in adversity, representing, as they do, everlasting life.

Tend your magical garden at this time. Bring in any herbs in pots, to shelter them from the worst of the weather. If your garden is more substantial, cover herbs and flowers with proper glass cloches, sheets of plastic, or straw for protection. But you can also generate magic in your garden, for all is not dead. This is the moment to clip your bay tree into pretty wintry shapes—stars, or spheres, or anything you please. Chant a spell while you work, because bay is sacred to Jupiter, and any cosmetic work you attend to on a sacred tree brings the favor of the gods. Ask favors that are in his domain: entertainment, a little extra prosperity, help with learning, travel, or law. Place a little walnut under each tree when you finish the wording of your spell-wish.

Tie ribbons to the branches of bare trees, and pretty up your festive greenery with ribbons of all colors. Choose appropriate colors for your hopes for the year ahead—pinks and reds for love and passion, greens and blues for security, health, and protection. Under one special tree—perhaps the one you like the most, or one that was planted for a special reason—place an outside candle in a weatherproof holder. Light it for an hour or so, saying personal things to someone who is (for any reason) out of reach but in your heart. Tell your most private wishes and desires to the earth itself, whose element belongs to winter. Afterward, be still for a few moments. This is a time to listen acutely to the almost inaudible breathing of the earth and the beating of your heart.

THE WINTER IRONING BASKET. Iron is very important in magic and was once regarded as sacred to the goddess Epona of the moon and horses, the Celtic deity equivalent to Diana, who is revered in witchcraft. Iron is a powerful metal that stores the knowledge of the "dark world"—which means not evil or negative magic but that which is hidden from us, in the realms where the earth sleeps. This is a product of the womb of Mother Earth.

A wondrous winter task recalls the magic of iron; it is connected with the old-fashioned pressing implement, reminding us that in the past, irons were indeed made from iron. The process of scenting your linen at this time of year with the aromas of the summer months buffets your sinking spirits and wafts gladness into the psyche. Don't underestimate the importance of the task or the lovely result of fragrancing your clothes in this way. When roses and lavender are diluted into distilled water for the ironing, you are indeed recalling the energy of the sun and producing magical effects from the iron itself. By all means, use commercial linen sprays, but if at all possible make your own, for no commercial product quite reaches linen kissed in winter by your own preparation.

Use 5 drops each of rose and lavender oil with 3 drops of rosemary oil and 2 drops of bergamot oil; add to 2 fl. oz. distilled water, blend well, and add to the water chamber of your iron. The resulting scent will help to counter cigarette smells, laundry chemicals, and bacteria, and will lift your spirits majestically above the gray winter skies. If you are ironing for a love date, increase the rose quantity to 8 drops, and omit the rosemary. There is a real property in these flower oils, but a magical one, too. All of them heal magically and all attract "butterflies" in the best sense: in other words, the goddess attends you. Always iron your clothes or linen in this way on an important day/date for luck from above—and add a pink ribbon around the handle of the iron if you are meeting your lover.

You can boost the iron's gifts with a swag made up in late fall from the last rosemary and lavender. Tie it with a purple ribbon and hang it upside down in your linen closet, where it will discourage insects as well as negativity. Always scent your sheets in this way if you like to sleep with romance.

PAYING HONOR WITH THE WHITE ROSE. There is a tale of a ritual from times long past which I love, and which derives from my Italian family. It tells of a family of good people who had fallen on hard times, but in the bleak winter they gathered up all the remaining roses in the garden and laid them out as follows. Their blessings following this ritual were manifold. You might try this to cheer your own heart in the chilly days and see afterward what luck is attracted to you. Indeed, something surprising always seems to happen....

Go into the garden or a park or public place where you can find a statue dedicated to a lady. Traditionally this was Diana, the lady of the bow, but any female statue will draw pleasure from the sleeping goddess. No matter how poor the weather (best of all, if it is snowing), adorn the statue with a little ivy or greenery and a few white roses. If you have no roses you may use hellebores if you have them growing in your garden (though be careful of their toxicity, and wash your hands well at the end). Scatter a ring of drops of rose oil or rosewater around the base of the statue and say: "*Lovely goddess of the bow [or lovely lady in marble or metal, etc.], you who wake in the starry heavens after the pale sun sinks in the winter sky, with the moon glimmering on your brow; lovely lady, who recalls your sisters sleeping in the earth, and who has known the days of nymphs and music here around you in warmer times; most gracious and most beauteous lady, who knows the powers to endure, think but for an instant on me, and on those of us who are here now who take pleasure in adorning you, and returning your wintry state to a summer haven.*"

You should bow to the lady and then invite a woman friend who has been in distress or had a pressured time around to your home for a drink or some food. Show sisterly feeling and invite male friends as well, if you like. Give your friend a few white flowers—especially roses—to go home with. When you go to bed yourself, scatter a few white rose petals on your pillow.

Very soon, perhaps even by the morning, a sign of fortune will present itself to you, and to your friend.

THE
WITCH'S
WEEK

OF COURSE, EVERYONE KNOWS THAT MIDNIGHT IS THE "WITCHING HOUR"—THE BEST TIME TO PERFORM MAGIC—BECAUSE THE EARTH SLEEPS, YOUR MENTAL POWERS ARE AT THEIR MOST INTENSE, AND YOU ARE LEAST LIKELY TO BE DISTURBED. BUT CERTAIN DAYS OF THE WEEK ARE ALSO MORE PROPITIOUS FOR PARTICULAR MAGICAL CEREMONIES. IN EVERY LANGUAGE, THE NAMES OF THE DAYS OF THE WEEK CAN STILL BE TRACED BACK TO THE PAGAN DEITIES WHOSE POWERS WERE SYNONYMOUS WITH THE ENERGY OF EACH INDIVIDUAL DAY. IF YOU WORK WITH THIS ANCIENT SPIRIT, AND HARMONIZE WITH THE FORCES THAT WERE SAID TO BE AT THEIR PEAK ON ANY ONE DAY, YOU MAY BE SURPRISED AT THE STRENGTH OF YOUR THOUGHT. MAGIC CAN BE DESCRIBED AS CHANGE WROUGHT THROUGH THE POWER OF THOUGHT AND THE PSYCHE, AND MAGIC WORKED ON ITS "TRUE" DAY OF THE WEEK WILL UTILIZE THE HIDDEN STORE OF THAT PSYCHE WITH GREATER POETRY.

MONDAY: THE MOON'S DAY. You need never dread that "Monday morning feeling" again if you approach the start of the working week with the right attitude. Honor the day, and it will treat you gently.

Monday is dedicated to the moon, and I have begun the week on this day (rather than Sunday) to commence with the power of female energy rather than the male energy of the sun.

Any magic you work on a Monday should incorporate the use of a moonstone and/or silver, and any spell you cast should properly concern the subjects of woman/motherhood (leave matters of love for Friday), the family, hearth and home, dreams and visions, or the sea.

On any Monday, whether you have magic to perform or not, start by honoring the day. Light a silvery, moonlight-colored candle, or one that favors the sea (blue-green or turquoise), and make a short wish for female strength and insight, and for kindness from the world around you. Do this for a few minutes before you leave the house in the morning.

A MONDAY SPELL FOR GOOD LUCK

Gather together a candle, as before, a pearl or moonstone, something silver, a white ribbon and a white flower—usually a rose or a poppy, although a little sprig of watercress (sacred to the moon) would do nicely. If you want even more power in your magic, honor the moon's rule over the sea and add a shell, a seahorse, a dish of salt, or any other seaside connection you have, such as a boat, pebbles, or driftwood.

Work early in the morning or late at night, perhaps in the comfort of your bedroom. Place your items around the candle and light it; close your eyes and envisage your desired goal. Speak some words of feminine entreaty to Diana, goddess of the moon, then smile or laugh and extinguish the flame. If you have held the thought clearly in your heart and head for a few moments, luck and power will be reflected in your life.

TUESDAY: THE DAY OF MARS, GOD OF WAR. Never as exciting as Thursday or Friday, nor as difficult to rise from bed for as Monday, Tuesday is often felt to be unimportant. Magically, however, this is the day for going into action, resolving (or initiating) matters of conflict, and dealing with matters of sexuality.

Tuesday also rules hunting, masculinity, physical strength and courage, lust, and issues concerned with fieriness. Honeysuckle and opals are sacred to the rites of Tuesday, especially if the opal is flecked with "fire," but a carnelian (bloodstone), a red ruby, or a garnet can also be used.

Tuesday is an appropriate day for working a love spell if a lack of physical consummation has been the problem. First, make up a blend of scented oils: add a few drops of black pepper and jasmine or vanilla essential oils to 1 fl. oz. alcohol, and leave for 48 hours. On a Tuesday evening, light a red candle girdled with a red ribbon with your lover's name "sealed" to it with sealing wax. Surround yourself in red light, and imagine it penetrating your erogenous zones. Spray a little peppery scent on your chest near your heart. You will now ooze with extraordinary sensual charm and confidence. You could also massage a little jasmine oil into your ankles to spark your wild side.

A Plea for Strength

Perhaps you are a gentle soul, steeling yourself to say something important but difficult to someone, and you feel it may require more aggression than you normally have. At such a moment, you can invoke the gods of war to lend you the strength for a combat—even if it is a gentle-hearted one.

On a Tuesday morning, gather together a red flower, some honeysuckle, or a fresh radish, as well as a red stone or opal, and something made from iron or steel (this last to symbolize your determination to be flintier than usual). Place them in front of a red candle and light it. As you do so, address Mars (think of him as the handsome hunk seduced by Venus in the Botticelli painting if you find a pure war god unappealing), and ask him for the strength to tackle somebody about an issue that concerns you. Close your eyes, and see yourself powerfully addressing your "foe" and having "the last word"—which stands for the final enchantment. Blow out your candle and utter a quick thanks.

You must contrive to have the words out and said within a very short time, preferably that very day. If you have properly imagined yourself girded for "war," you will soon find that you take command of the situation and achieve the result you desire.

WEDNESDAY: THE DAY OF WODEN. I have always found children born on a Wednesday to be especially lucky in their powers of speech and persuasion. The day is traditionally sacred to the all-powerful Woden (or Odin), the father god and magician, charmer with words, who is also related to the Roman god Mercury and the Greek Hermes, both also magical messengers and magicians.

Wednesday rules both conscious and unconscious mental prowess: study, spoken messages, letters and communications of all kinds, telepathy, divination, and predictions. Sacred to Wednesday are the hazel tree, mulberry, and lily-of-the-valley, the gems sapphire and amethyst, the metal mercury (quicksilver), and the color violet.

For luck in your studies, or with anything concerning the giving of a speech or a talk, do the following on a Wednesday morning. Honor the deity in your own simple words, place one of the above flowers or a hazelnut beside a very small violet-colored candle, and ask for extra power and sway in the day ahead. Light the candle and make a very quick wish, seeing the task before you melt into pleasure and achieving pure joy. Blow out the flame, and wave your hand once through the smoke. Success is yours for the taking!

SENDING A MESSAGE BY MAGICAL MEANS

No need to go to the bother of mailing letters when you can communicate in this way. On a Wednesday after 7:00 p.m., send a mental message to a friend you want to contact, or imagine saying simple words you find difficult to phrase face-to-face, perhaps to heal a quarrel or express emotion.

Put a photo of the recipient in front of you, and invoke Woden, or Mercury, or Hermes. Light a violet-colored candle, and use a hazelnut or rod to forge contact between you and the gods and the person you would speak with. Roll the hazelnut or rod in your hand and wave this same hand or wand over the picture. Speak the words you wish to say very gently; you might simply articulate: "*Please get in touch*," or "*I'm sorry we quarreled,*" or "*Could you express your feelings for me a little more?*" or something of this nature. Blow out the candle only after you have phrased some words of thanks to the deity of Wednesday. Leave the hazelnut near the photo of your friend. You will shortly find your thoughts have been communicated to the one you wish to contact.

THURSDAY: THE DAY OF THOR. A very lucky day, belonging to the Roman Jupiter, the Greek Zeus, and the Norse and Teutonic equivalent Thor ("the thunderer").

Dedicate this day to issues concerning luck and prosperity, legal matters, high honors, and all forms of material expansion. Thor, Zeus, and Jupiter are all connected with the oak and thus with mistletoe, most prized by the Druids. This was the day thought to have the greatest power and connection with the strongest gods until supplanted by Sunday, when the Emperor Constantine pronounced it as the day of the Lord. However, Thursday is still regarded as the most potent day for witchcraft—and it is the child born on this day who is said to have "far to go."

Sacred to Thursday is anything connected with oak leaves and trees, acorns, or mistletoe; also storms and heavy rain—a storm on a Thursday is sent by the gods and should be reveled in, or danced in, Gene Kelly-style! Powerfully scented red carnations and borage (aptly called "starflower") are also sacred to Thursday, as well as the metal tin—though when addressing the gods, it should be done with white gold (on Sunday use yellow gold). Opinion is divided as to whether the gemstone should be diamond or topaz, but I prefer the more precious stone because of the ancient tradition of this day being one of prosperity and financial power.

TO ATTRACT SUCCESS AND PROSPERITY

Thursday, then, is the key day for material matters. If you need a new job, or want promotion, light a green or gold candle every Thursday for a month, starting with a waning moon to magnetize bad luck away, then on the waxing moon to attract a new and positive contract or opportunity to you. Have a purification bath filled with oak leaves, do anything with an oak leaf or tree that honors it, and burn woody incense. Cut a golden bough of mistletoe to invoke the wisdom of the gods to help you in a new life, and even after Christmas, retain a few leaves or berries somewhere precious, which was traditionally in a white cloth. If you really want divine intervention, you should cut some mistletoe with a golden blade—though admittedly, this could be tricky. Keep a little gold chain with the sprig instead, for gold is sacred to the gods, whereas iron keeps supernatural energy at bay. Most importantly, sleep on a diamond—the tiniest one will do—and wear a little diamond until your luck waxes. Always honor the day, and look for that huge planet Jupiter in the night sky.

FRIDAY: SACRED TO FREYA. She is the Norse love goddess, a creature of charm and sensuous fertility, also called Frigg, whose equivalent is Venus or Aphrodite; the name of Venus finds echoes in the French and Italian names for Friday—Vendredi and Venerdi.

This is the perfect day for a love spell, but also for other Venusian attributes—spells and rituals for pleasure, perfume making and buying, issues concerned with beauty and eroticism, with music and the arts.

Sacred to Friday is the rose, personal emblem of the love goddess. Pink or red are traditional love roses, whereas white is chaste and suits the moon. Extra special potency comes on a Friday from a wild rose. On a Friday, make a simple shrine to honor the love goddess—place a single stem or odd number of roses in a vase, and drop in a small crystal or semiprecious stone. Do this if you would like to bring added joys, brighter pleasures, a more artistic spark, or luck in love on a Friday.

The sacred gemstone of Venus and Friday is the beautiful emerald, symbolic of love and success, or alternatively it could be tourmaline, symbolic of hope. Worn on a Friday, either will bestow luck and lend you flashes of imagination and sensuality.

AN EASY LOVE SPELL FOR A FRIDAY

This can be performed in five minutes at either end of the day, around 6:00–7:00 a.m. or p.m. Light a pink or rose-scented candle, address your goddess, ask for her friendship and blessings today, and express to her in a few simple words any worry or doubt or problem you are experiencing in the area of love or emotional partnerships. Ask her to find you a space in the day to help you clear up this difficulty with your loved one, ending with the words: "*So mote it be.*" Blow out the candle very fast, like a wish on a birthday cake, then see if you can spot Venus in the morning or evening sky, a very twinkly blue star. Now set out for the day or evening ahead feeling warmly humorous and very confident.

SATURDAY: SATURN'S DAY. For most of us, Saturday is the start of the weekend, yet Saturn is the taskmaster of the gods, whose concerns are hard work, common sense, providing sensibly, and securing property. So perhaps it makes some sense that we now spend so much time doing our household chores on Saturdays.

This is certainly the day for property transactions and magically is an ideal day to move to a new home. Spells to find houses or protect your home should be performed on this day. Rowan trees are often used in property magic, so a rowan twig bound to a house key and a dark green or earth-brown candle, lit and dedicated to Saturn, will ensure security in your home.

The snowdrop empathizes with Saturday. Saturn was the lord of death and ruler of the night, including the dark of midwinter. The snowdrop is the first consolation that Saturn brings back something from what was taken. Always view snowdrops with a sense of replenishment, a reminder that we can recover from waning times in our affairs through hard work and dedication. Hellebores (Christmas roses), comfrey, and ivy are also sacred to Saturn.

A RITUAL FOR MOVING INTO A NEW HOME

If possible, choose a waxing moon for the move, for you are growing into something positive.

Have one of your new door keys silver-plated by a key-cutter (or you could spray it silver or cover it in silver foil). Show the key to the moon the night before you turn it in the lock, and ask for blessings and happy dreams inside your dwelling. On the day you move in, place a strand of pink, green, or white ribbon across the threshold and tie a fragment of it around the top of the key, too. Use a pair of scissors to cut through the ribbon with your loved one(s), and make a wish. Take the silver key and place it inside a shell near a candle or fireplace, and burn some incense just near it—pine or benzoin (or orange if you're newly married)—to cast out negative thoughts and usher in strong new ones. Light the fire or candle, and see a happy home and hearth enveloping you. Ask for protection, especially from fire. Then, restore the key (with the ribbon) to a lucky place, and use it thereafter only symbolically.

Your house move would be completely blessed if you could plant a rowan tree or a willow in the garden or in a large pot, asking that the gods smile on your space.

SUNDAY: DAY OF THE BRIGHT SUN. Originally sacred to Apollo and the sun and thereafter to God, this is the day of maximum power, and should be commemorated with fire.

Sunday is the day for general spells, for ideas concerning people in charge, such as world leaders and politicians, or employers on the grand scale. It is also connected with health and healing, friendship in the broadest sense, but also with holidays and fun. Work some magic on a Sunday if you need time off or want to plan a feast such as a wedding or party. This will ensure that your celebration goes like a rocket. This is also the day to think thoughts and make wishes that concern men and women around you in positions of power or authority.

Sunday is the best day to honor the sunshine hours, especially in the garden, and to make time for personal peace, and rest. We must remember this, for increasingly our leisure hours are swallowed up with work of some kind. Even if you must work on a Sunday, make one hour for rest, peace and honoring the sun—the more so if the day itself is gray.

Sunday's colors are sunshine yellow, orange, yellow gold, and even the colors of the rainbow. Its gem is the potent ruby, sometimes the peridot. The flowers are many, all flowers of joy and healing. They include sunflowers and marigolds, but also the spice saffron, the yellow-hued heartsease (pansy), and the celandine. More recently, citrus flowers and even the tiger lily have been connected with the sun and Sunday.

If you would like to emit an aura of radiant confidence and happiness, choose a Sunday to work this ritual. Choose a candle from the sunshine color spectrum, a citrus scent, and a tall, yellow flower, and bring them together early on a Sunday. Toast the sun with citrus juice, and make a vow to honor both the spirit of rest and the spirit of solar power in some way today. Tie a yellow ribbon around your wrist to harness the energy from your short ritual.

CONCLUSION: THIS BRINGS US TO YOUR ULTIMATE LESSON. Your odyssey will have sparked many ideas of your own, and you will have your own signature sense of what it means to be a "witch."

You will have discovered your own ways of working magic, and you should have found the methods that work best for you personally. If you have woven your dreams and magic wisely and well across the year, you will have strengthened your awareness of the world around you, taken charge of many matters in your life, and added fairy dust to the lives of many friends and loved ones—even some who may think you a little strange! THAT'S MAGIC! *Blessed Be.*

A Glossary of Terms Used in This Book

Throughout the book you will come across various terms within spell working that may not be clear to you unless you have read my earlier spell books. Here is a brief explanation of such terms.

"Charging with Power." This will arise when you are asked to "charge" a magnet or metal object, even a candle, with "power" or light drawn from the sun or from the moon.

Hold the object in the light, and vividly imagine the energy from the particular source entering into the object and filling it with particles of light and positivity. If you are asked to draw the power of the sun or moon, or even the light from candles, into yourself to boost your own sense of positivity and energy, you must concentrate and try to "feel" the heat gradually filling your body—from the tip of your toes to the top of your head—so that you can then draw on this special celestial power.

"Breathing in" Scent or Color. This is to send greater force with your magic. Throughout the book you will find particular scents and colors tied to individual subjects, which will usually involve a colored candle, sometimes also scented.

Inhale the "feeling" of the color, along with the scent if appropriate, by powerfully imagining the color entering your heart, lungs, head, and chest, spreading gradually through your body, diffusing a glowing, good feeling as it does so. This alters your vibratory rate and attunes you to the power of that particular color. Scent, of course, strengthens the effect.

"Cleansing." This might be applied to your magic working space, your home, or a car, or in fact you yourself. It is a procedure of purification achieved mentally; sometimes, again, with scent as a backup. Imagine white light pouring forth from the source of the sun, or a fire, or anything that you can associate with

positive power and strength (this may again be a simple candle!). Concentrate your thoughts on the light until you can almost feel your own temperature rise, and then you must direct this light and heat to the area required. If the energy is required to cleanse a space, see the heat and light eddying around the area like a great whirlpool of white energy. Prolong the feeling for a few minutes—although you may feel quite drained later!

Sending a Mental Message. You may be asked to envision someone, then send them a simple message in your magic working, particularly in love magic or if someone is ill or away from you.

You will first have chosen appropriate colors/scents to work with, and sometimes music helps you to feel closer to someone special if it is a shared song or poignant piece. Then, imagine their face as vividly as you can, preferably at a happy moment; freeze their smile and look as though directed totally at you, then quietly and calmly imagine you are touching their body, or hands, or face, truly as if they were right with you. When you have the feeling that "contact" has been made, say your simple words (out loud, if you prefer) and imagine their face/eyes/smile recognizing what you have said. Send them a feeling of sweetness (perhaps like a gentle kiss) and then imagine them surrounded by a real, physical, powerful halo of light. Your message is complete.

"Embracing" the Moon, Sun, etc. This may be to say "thank you" after a spell has worked, or it may be to draw a feeling of warmth into your physical body before working magic.

Literally hold your arms outstretched and imagine hugging the moon, stars, sun, or a light source like candles or fire. Feel love for the world, banish anger and distress, fill up your tank on the vastness of the world and all in it that's good.

INDEX